What people are
Living C

D0509363

"Joe Cipriano and I are kindred spirits. We both began our broadcast careers on radio as teenagers in the 1970s. *Living On Air* isn't only a wonderfully written stroll down Joe's Memory Lane. It's also helped me find the map to my own. Thanks, Joe."

--Tom Bergeron, Host "Dancing with the Stars"

"Joe Cipriano has been our guy in the booth for over 14 years on shows like the *Emmys, Grammys, Blockbuster Awards,* and more. We've been through a lot together in doing live television, and his stories in this book are funny, charming and a great inside look into the challenges and the incredible fun that we've had along the way. Joe's the best!!!"

-- Ken Ehrlich, Producer Emmy Awards, Grammy Awards

"Only one voice was truly synonymous with Fox's groundbreaking comedies like *Married with Children, The Simpsons,* and *In Living Color* and that voice belonged to Joe Cipriano. His distinctive style was the perfect complement to the fresh, youthful, alternative, and outrageous attitude that came to define the fourth network."

--Sandy Grushow, Former Chairman, Fox TV

"People who watch my show, *Iron Chef America,* hear my friend Joe Cipriano whenever I speak. Joe is my voice man!! His book is filled with great stories. It's a funny, warm, and entertaining read."

--Iron Chef Masaharu Morimoto

"When you think about voices that stick in your head, names like Joe Cipriano come to mind. Joe's energy, unique style, and recognizable voice bring products to life. And take it from me, no one says 'Sunday at 8/7 Central' better than Joe Cipriano!"

--Rick Dees, National Radio Host

"Joe has an amazing voice, a great sense of humor, & a big heart ... No wonder he's the best in the biz! A great read from my great friend."

--Ellen K, "On Air with Ryan Seacrest"

"At last, a brilliant, emotional, and insightful look into the world of voiceover, from one of the industries best. I loved it! Rock On, Joe and Annie!"

--Michael Damian, Actor, Director, Musician

"Success is all about cherishing relationships along the way and the wonderful support of friends and colleagues. I'm happy to be along for the ride on Joe's 'On Air' journeys across America."

--Rita Vennari, President SBV Talent Agency

"Davey, Tom, Joe ... or more simply Cip. It's time to celebrate the fact we live 'In a world' where a scrawny kid from Watertown can rise to the top of his industry and have a cee-ment pond, a great wife, and amazing children. All well deserved my friend."

--Steve Feica, Former WWCO News Director and
Associated Press Editor

"*Living On Air,* truly mirrors the winning personality of the unusually gifted Joe Cipriano and the intriguing backstage lifestyle of live radio and voiceover announcing. And like Joe's dazzling smile and exalting vocal expression, *Living On Air* will lift you up with compelling anecdotes and life lessons that remind us to live well and go after our dreams. It's a book full of heart and fun."

--Joan Baker, Voice Actor & Coach, Author, "Secrets of Voice Over Success"

"I got to know Joe Cipriano during the creation of the Don LaFontaine Voice Over Lab at the SAG Foundation. Joe has a knack for gathering people together for a worthy cause and Joe brought them in, in droves. His energy and his commitment to making the Lab a reality was impressive. His book is filled with the same energy, along with funny and endearing stories about his life and remarkable career in voice over."

--JoBeth Williams, Film, TV, Stage Actress and President SAG Foundation

"What an informative and entertaining read from one of the best in the business…hilarious and poignant"

--Paul Pape, Actor, Co-Founder Don LaFontaine Voice Over Lab

"*Living On Air* is a charming read about how an ordinary boy from a small town in CT managed to achieve an extraordinary career in the world of radio and voice over. Joe Cipriano is an inspiration for anyone who has a dream. While this is not a how-to book, it is easy to trace the steps that led to his incredible success. Joe's tenacity, dedication and sheer passion opened doors for him because when you work that hard, you are always at the right place at the right time. His encounters with major stars are L.O.L. funny. Joe's sunny disposition can be felt throughout and as a result, I found myself smiling from the very first page right on through to the last."

--Fay Ann Lee, Actress, Singer, Writer, Director

"Joe Cipriano is a perfect example of what happens when luck, opportunity and preparedness collide. Every candid, uncensored story reveals more of his amazing heart, persistent nature, risk-taking spirit, self confidence, and unwavering faith. What an honor to go on this inspiring and touching roller coaster ride with Joe and Ann, they're the best partners in every way! We love you!"

--Stacey J. Aswad and Chuck Duran, Hosts VO Buzz Weekly

"I enjoy Cip's romanticizing of radio and his stories of what it's like to literally grow up on the air in front of thousands of listeners during radios personality days. If you're someone who loves the broadcasting industry as much as I do then you'll love the stories in this book. Great job Cip!"

--Sean "Hollywood" Hamilton, NYC / Syndicated Radio Personality

Back Cover Photo credit: Ryan Stephenson

Cover Design by Velin@Perseus-Design.com

Living
ON AIR

Adventures in Broadcasting

Wendy —
Wishing you all the
Best in your VO career!

by Joe Cipriano
with Ann Cipriano

Joe C 4/23/14

Living on Air

Published by Joe Cipriano Promos Inc.

ISBN 978-0-9910126-8-8

Copyright © 2013 by Joe Cipriano

Cover design by Velin@Perseus-Design.com

For more information on this book and the author visit:
www.livingonairbook.com

To Dayna and Alex

Living
ON AIR

Contents

Introduction

I have an incredible job. It pays more than I ever thought I could earn, it's fun, it's creative, and I've met the most wonderful people, all through my work. I like to think it takes someone with extraordinary talent and remarkable good looks to get to where I am today, but the truth is it takes hard work, determination, and a lotta luck. I'm told my good looks didn't help one bit.

I am a voice-over actor. Some folks give me a blank look when I tell them what I do, so I describe it by saying I'm a television announcer. Mostly I voice network promos, "Monday on CBS," "Sunday on an all-new Simpsons," that kind of stuff, but I've also worked on movie trailers, live television shows, game shows, commercials, radio, you name it, I've done it. I was a kid from a small town, David Joseph Cipriano, without a college education, and yet I became one of the top people in my profession. People always stop to ask me if they can learn to do what I do and that's why I wanted to share my story. Through trial and error, successes and more error, I found my voice. Whatever your dream is, I hope my journey can help you find your voice, too.

As much as I love what I do, it should come with a warning label: "This job may be hazardous to your health." There are unbelievable highs and terrible lows. It has the ability to turn your stomach around and upside down, a little bit like taking a ride on a roller coaster, without a seat belt. And the truth is, I have

been unceremoniously kicked off this ride, more often than I like to remember. The worst time happened without any warning, when most people thought I had it all.

I suppose it helps that I'm a positive guy. I'm always looking for luck to come my way. I would much rather live each day thinking good things are going to happen instead of bad. Not that I don't get disheartened, because of course, that happens, too. But I have been able to reinvent myself every time I hit that unexpected dive on the roller coaster. And I'm convinced my positive attitude has helped make my dreams come true.

Whenever people ask for my advice, I always tell them to follow their heart. Take that risk, but hold on to your day job while you go for it. If there is one thing I've learned, whatever gig I have at the moment isn't mine to keep, it's just on loan, until somebody else comes along. It goes away, it comes back, and repeats that cycle over and over again. That arbitrary aspect of my job reminds me of when I was a kid, picking dandelions out in the yard. There's that white, puffy ball at the top of the stem I used to blow on, and the seeds spread out all over the lawn. Holding on to a voice-over gig is a little like trying to catch all of those seeds, scattering in the wind.

My dad used to tell me, if you love your job, you'll never work a day in your life. So far I'm still here, holding on to my seat, having the time of my life. I hope you enjoy the ride.

SUMMER OF '69

WWCO was a small-time radio station that hungered for a big-time sound. It was the hub of our world of entertainment for everything new and exciting that happened around my hometown, Oakville, Connecticut. For as far back as I can remember, my mom listened to that station every single day of her life. Each morning as I got ready for school, I woke up to the smell of fresh coffee brewing in the air and the sound of my mom humming along to a song on the air. We used to have a tan General Electric clock radio that sat on top of our refrigerator, always tuned in to 1240 on your AM dial. Coming downstairs, I'd walk into our warm kitchen on a cold morning as the soundtrack of my young life played out on that local Top 40 radio station.

The deejays at C-O were the most famous celebrities I could ever hope to meet. They didn't all look like movie stars, but they had a confidence and authority that was irresistible to me. They were talented guys who really came alive during those few hours they were on the air. I could feel their passion through our radio at home, and even out of the speaker in our car. It was contagious, but it was the kind of disease I wanted to catch.

It seemed to me that everybody who worked at the station was part of a team, one big family, and if you were a deejay, you were the star. All the girls wanted to date him. I wanted to be him.

WWCO was owned by Merv Griffin, the talk-show host, singer, actor, and media mogul. He bought it in 1965, the first link in his radio chain, then sold it eight years later. The AM station played my favorite music, all the popular hits of the time, while the FM station played country songs. I didn't even know there was an FM signal. Hardly anyone else did either. At that time, all anyone ever listened to was AM Top 40 radio.

I was 14 years old when I started hanging out at the station on weekends, in that summer of '69. That was the year Neil Armstrong walked on the moon, the Woodstock Music Festival took over Max Yasgur's farm in upstate New York, and Charles Manson went on a killing spree in the Hollywood Hills. My parents and their friends talked about a generation gap while most of their kids talked about a revolution. Meanwhile, I was going through my own rebellion, more of an evolution instead of a revolution. I had enough self-confidence, ambition, and arrogance to think that if I worked hard enough, I could make anything happen. With my heart set on becoming a deejay, that's all I talked about, hoped for, and counted on coming true.

I was inspired by the NASA program, the Kennedys, the Civil Rights Movement, even the Smothers Brothers television show. Everything that was going on around the world motivated me to start making my own dream a reality. While my friends were focused on getting their homework done for the next day, I worked on planning my future. I had no idea how to get started. The only thing I could think of was to call my favorite disc jockey at my favorite radio station.

Jerry Wolf had the afternoon shift at WWCO. There was no one on the radio like him. He was funny, smart, quick, irreverent, creative, everything I hoped to be. He had this saying, his signature

phrase that everybody knew, "This is Jerry Wolf, rappin' on you and pumpin' out too what you're pumpin' in on the request lines!" I wasn't even sure what it meant but it was original and it sounded cool. He talked so fast it felt like each word was shot out of his mouth like a machine gun. I would imitate him at home over and over again until I could talk just as fast. That must have driven my folks crazy.

I saw Jerry's picture once at the Naugatuck Valley Mall in a print advertisement for a mod clothing store called Chess King. From that moment on his image became my vision of what every deejay should look like. He was tall, thin, with long dark hair down to his shoulders, and a full beard trimmed close to his face. As soon as school let out at the end of that year, I decided to make my move. I picked up the phone in our hallway upstairs, stretched the cord as far as it would reach into my bedroom, closed the door, and sat on my bed at the window. I practiced what I was going to say, then started dialing the WWCO request line. Two days later, I finally got through.

"Hey man, this is Jer at 1240 C-O. What can I do for ya?"

All keyed up from waiting so long, I blurted out what I wanted to say in one breath, faster than Jerry's own radio rap.

"Hi, Jerry? Uh, my name is Dave Cipriano and I really like WWCO and I love your show and someday I want to be a disc jockey too and I was wondering if there is any chance if some day I can come down to the radio station and meet you and see what the station is like…some day?"

"Well, cool man, that'd be really cool. Yeah, we can have you come down. Hey listen little man, just call this number and we'll set it up for ya."

After I hung up the phone I sat calmly, staring out the window, for about one second before I let out a yell. I could hardly believe what just happened. I had actually talked to Jerry Wolf, my idol, the coolest deejay on the radio. I played the conversation over and over in my head. Right away I got back on the phone to call every one of my friends. I couldn't wait to tell them that I talked to that guy on the radio. Even better, that he invited me to come down to the station.

During the school year my mom had to practically drag me out of bed every morning but the day I was scheduled to visit C-O I shot off the mattress like I was launched out of an Apollo rocket. Dad was at work and my mom didn't drive, so I had to take the bus from Oakville to downtown Waterbury. The bus stop was in front of the only movie theater in town, called the Mighty Oak. That's where I saw all of my favorite films, like Steve McQueen's "Bullitt" and "Planet of the Apes" with Charlton Heston. In the bright light of day I noticed the Mighty Oak looked kind of small and insignificant.

It was about a 20-minute ride to Exchange Place, the bus station downtown in the center of Waterbury. Across the street was a large rectangle of grass called The Green, our city park. Summer had grabbed hold of Connecticut. I saw businessmen on park benches sweating through their suits, women in pageboy haircuts and polka-dot dresses, teenagers stretched out on blankets on the grass with their hair hanging down and their transistor radios turned up. I heard snatches of 1240 WWCO in the air as I walked past a diner on South Main Street. There was a sign in the window advertising a Cheeseburger Deluxe Blue Plate Special for 35 cents and a chocolate shake for an extra 16 pennies. A few doors down was an old brick building, six stories high with a wood and glass door out front. That was my destination, 65 Bank Street.

I stopped for a second to catch my breath, then yanked open the door. There was a long hallway with dark wood floors and my eyes had to adjust to the changing light. At the end of the hall was an elevator lit by a single bare light bulb. An older man with thin grey hair was sitting on a metal stool just inside. He was wearing dark wool pants, so out of place on a hot summer day, a white short-sleeved shirt, and a rag of a skinny black tie around his neck. As I walked over to the elevator he looked up from his newspaper and snuffed out a half-smoked cigarette. I pulled out a wrinkled piece of paper that was stuffed into my back pocket and checked out the few words I had scribbled down to make sure I was headed to the right place.

"Excuse me, sir, I'm here to see Jerry Wolf. Can you please take me up to the fifth floor?"

"Well, this thing don't go sideways, kid, so we only got one choice."

I stepped in as he reached past me to shut a large metal door, then tugged sideways on an accordion gate until it clicked shut. He pulled on a long-armed lever and the elevator jerked upwards towards number five. As we moved higher I heard muffled music coming through the walls, getting louder with each floor. He guided the elevator to a smooth stop, slid back the gate, and on the inside of the metal door was a big number five stenciled in white paint. That door was the last obstacle to the unknown adventure waiting on the other side for me, a kid from a small town, with big dreams. Once that door opened I was positive my life was going to change forever.

The first thing my eyes settled on was a pretty girl in a pink paisley miniskirt standing next to the reception desk.

"Hi! You must be David. Welcome to WWCO."

She was about ten years older than me and she had on the shortest, totally mod micro-mini-est skirt I had ever seen. Her long dark hair was parted in the middle with two blond streaks on either side of her face. Her wrists were loaded with a bunch of bright-colored plastic bracelets and when she reached to shake my hand, they clattered up and down with each arm pump. I followed her towards a small lobby with my eyes riveted on her extremely short skirt. With each step I could see the line of her pantyhose where it changed to a darker color and I kept watching and waiting for her skirt to go higher. When we got to the lobby she stopped short, turned back around and tapped her toe on the floor. Startled, I nearly bumped into her.

"Do you like this, David?" Uh oh, I thought, did she catch me looking at her legs? But thankfully I was wrong. Looking down at the floor she said, "Mr. Griffin had this made just for us when he bought the radio station. Isn't it fab?"

Right in the middle of the floor, set out in black tile under her white patent leather boots, were the words: "WWCO 1240 on your radio dial." Next to that was a picture of a classic microphone emblazoned on the white floor. Did I think it was fab? Hell, yes. I had never before seen a custom-made sign built right into the floor. That was cool. Next, she took me on a quick tour around the office.

There were gold records on the walls in big picture frames and magazines called Billboard, Sixteen, and Tiger Beat all over the place. There was a knockout secretary named Dorsie Dues who typed up the log of commercials that ran on the air. She had legs that went on forever. We walked past women in tight T-shirts, pounding away on their typewriters, and salesmen yakking on

the phone wearing big ties under big collars. I saw a sports coat hanging on the back of a guy's chair with a badge on the pocket that said, "WWCO A Merv Griffin Station." All of that action was enough to make my head spin, but suddenly it was overshadowed by the sound of the Top 40 hit "In the Year 2525" by Zager and Evans pouring out of a speaker mounted on the wall. As the song began to fade, the voice of Waterbury's favorite deejay shouted out over those last few notes.

"Zager and Evans man, 'In the Year 2525'…phew, that's a long time from now. I hope chicks are still wearing minis 'cause if not, I mean, what's the point?"

A female chorus of peppy, sweet harmonies sang out cheerfully, "Double-You-Double-You…SEE OHHH," then the opening bars of the next song instantly started up, "Everyday People" by Sly and the Family Stone.

"WWCO man! Jer' Wolf rappin' on you and pumpin' out TOO what your pumpin' in on the request lines, 'cause we're all in this together man, can you dig it, you, me, and Sly Stone… we're just 'Everyday People'!"

BAM, Sly Stone's voice cut through immediately, loud and clear, right on beat, singing the opening lyric.

I was pulled back into the room by the sound of a young woman's voice.

"So, are you ready to go upstairs to the studio to meet Jerry?"

"I sure am!" I was curious about everything I saw that day and innocent enough to say whatever was on my mind. I had plenty of questions but there was one that to me was the most important.

"Do you get to talk to Jerry and the rest of the deejays all the time?"

"Yeah, I sure do."

Wow.

From the office we walked towards a flight of worn-down wooden stairs. We climbed up to the sixth floor, into another hallway. Straight ahead was a room with a couple of green vinyl chairs and a matching sofa with shiny chrome legs. There was a table up against the wall with a half-empty mug of something sitting on top, next to a leftover cheeseburger, and an ashtray full of cigarette butts.

"That's the jock lounge," said my miniskirted tour guide. "That's where the deejays all hang out before and after their shows."

I stuck my head through the door and smiled, thinking how I might look sitting in one of those chairs. It was like a clubhouse for grownups. I didn't care about the stains on the cushions or the trash on the floor. It was perfect. We walked down the hallway between two huge indoor windows on both sides of us. I turned to the right and through the glass there was a guy sitting behind a microphone wearing a cowboy hat. That sure wasn't Jerry Wolf.

"This is the FM studio. That's our country music station."

What language was she speaking? Who the heck listens to FM radio? Or country music? I turned around to ask about Jerry when my eyes drifted over through the window on the other side of the hallway and there he was, looking exactly like the picture I had seen at the mall. Jerry Wolf. He had just finished saying something on the radio and he was taking off his sleek black headphones when he looked up and caught sight of the two of

us in the hallway. He flashed a smile and waved for us to come inside his lair.

"David, this is Jerry Wolf!"

"Hey man, how ya doin'? So you wanna be a deejay someday, huh?"

"I sure do! Wow, this is really something!"

Jerry leaned over a stack of records, stuck out his hand for a shake and I grabbed on to keep from falling over. There was so much to see I hardly knew where to start. The AM studio was one step up from the hall floor, a floating room with a huge heavy door and thick soundproof walls. It was like stepping onto a concert stage. The first thing that hit me was how cool everything was, the feel of the room and even the temperature. While the rest of the building made do with window fans to beat the heat, the studio was air-conditioned to a chilly 68 degrees.

There were pictures of rock stars on the walls, along with posters of my favorite bands. I saw Led Zeppelin's debut LP, with the black-and-white image of the Hindenburg exploding. Next to that was Tommy James and the Shondells' psychedelic cover for "Crimson and Clover." There were forty-five rpm records everywhere, and metal racks with plastic cartridges in each slot. The music was booming in my ears. Jerry stood in the middle of the room with all the equipment surrounding him in a U shape. He was captain of the ship running the control board, two turntables, tape machines, his microphone, and other stuff I didn't know what to call. When I glanced at the telephone it looked like it was on fire, every single number glowed with a blinking white light.

Jerry was constantly in motion, a frenetic mass of energy

rappin' and pumpin' his way through the afternoon. He wore a long-sleeved shirt rolled up at his wrists with a buttoned-up vest and dark blue jeans. I could tell he cared about his looks, but in a good way, like the way he cared about his job. He pulled up a chair for me and I sat down right next to him.

"Hey man, hold on a second, I gotta go on the radio."

He popped on his earphones. They seemed to be made out of the same Bakelite plastic as our kitchen radio back home. I saw the word "Clevite" stamped on the side and made a mental note to remember that name. Headphones in place, Jerry cranked up the volume of the studio speaker. It was incredibly loud, crisp, and clean. He watched the record go round on the turntable to his right then flipped a switch to turn on his microphone. As soon as he did that, the room went absolutely silent. The music was now blasting solely in Jerry's ears. He started tapping his foot, and shaking his whole body, and I could hear the music leaking out of his headphones. Then he started rapping to his radio listeners, telling everyone how hip the song was. At the same time he was doing that, he started up the next record on the other turntable. Over the intro of the new song he reminded his loyal multitude of sunbathing fans that it was "Time to turn so you just don't burn." He did his whole thing right in front of me and it was like listening to my transistor radio at home but it was all coming out of his mouth and I was like, FAR OUT! It was unbelievable.

I sat there for a little while longer until my personal tour guide came back to get me. At the end of my visit I guess Jerry saw the stars in my eyes, or maybe he saw a young kid who would help him with some of the work he wasn't fond of doing every week, because he asked me if I would like to come back.

"You know little man, I'm the music director here and it's a lotta work sorting through all the records and keeping the library straight. Why don't you come down on Saturdays and help me out? You can meet the other guys and I'll show you how all this stuff works."

That's exactly what I did every weekend for the rest of the summer. At home, before heading for the bus, I would grab my record case stuffed with forty-fives, along with my lunch, then head outside, giving one last look back because whenever I left the house, my mom always stood behind the screen door, waving at me. Every weekend Mom made me a fresh meatball grinder with her homemade sauce. At least that's what we called them. Where you live, they might be called hoagies or subs or maybe you don't name them at all, you're just content to eat them. Mom would cook up the meatballs while I was getting dressed, slather them onto some fresh Italian bread and wrap it up in aluminum foil. I could still feel the heat radiating out of the paper bag, even after I got off the bus downtown. I stayed at the station until ten or eleven at night, when my dad drove down to pick me up.

That whole summer I filed records, ripped news from the wire machines, ran out to pick up food for the deejays, answered phone calls, and basically did anything Jerry asked of me. I think if anyone had told me to clean the bathrooms, I would have done that, too. After his shift, Jerry always had to record a couple of commercials so he took me into the production room with him to show me how everything worked. He was a perfectionist in the booth, sometimes taking two or three hours to produce a spot until he was satisfied. As long as it took, I would watch and learn. He taught me how to thread the reel-to-reel tape and how to fire up the cart machines so I could run commercials. But the

best time of all was the very first day when he showed me how to cue up a record.

"Alright man, now I'm gonna show you how radio works, can ya dig it? How you play a jingle, start up a record, and how you talk over the intro of a song."

He sat me down and pulled a record out of its sleeve.

"You're gonna like this tune man. This is a cool record. It's the brand-new Rolling Stones single that we just started playin' today. It's called 'Honky Tonk Women.'"

He put the record on the turntable, picked up the needle, put it at the front of the record and flipped the switch. The huge turntable began to spin and the second you heard the cowbell at the beginning of "Honky Tonk Women" he said, "Okay, now we're gonna stop it right there," and he put his index finger on the record and started slipping it backwards to that first sound and then he brought it back another half turn after that. Next he pulled out an audio cart that had a label on it that said, "WWCO Jingle," and slipped it into the cart machine, pulling back a lever locking it in place. Then he said, "OK, so you do your rap on the microphone and then you hit the button on the cart machine that starts the jingle, 'Dubble-You-Dubble-You…SEE OHHH!' But you have to anticipate the end of them singing 'SEE OHHH' so you can start your record on time. Right around the time they're singing 'SEE,' you have to flip the switch to start that turntable spinning. By the time they sing 'OHHH' the turntable will have rotated a half turn to get up to speed and your song will start, bamm right after they finish singing. It's gotta go right into the song man, so timing is everything!"

Then it was my turn. I was excited and I wanted to get it just

right. I guess he understood because Jerry left me alone to figure it out on my own. It was the first time ever I was allowed to play with the equipment in the production room all by myself. I was just like the kid in the candy store. I pushed all the buttons, then turned up the music as loud as I could stand it. I spent at least one hour, maybe more, in the production room that day, doing my make-believe radio show. Jerry's wired-up energy rubbed off on me and I kept cueing up "Honky Tonk Women" until I destroyed the beginning of that record with cue burns. From that moment on, Jerry told me I could go into that studio whenever I wanted, to practice how to be a deejay. He even gave me my own reel of tape so I could record myself to take home later for a listen. I was living my dream.

Before I knew it, summer was nearly over. I was having so much fun, time flew right by. I packed up my forty-fives, grabbed my reel-to reel tapes, and wondered how I would get through school without being able to visit the radio station anymore. Worst of all, I had to say goodbye to Jerry Wolf.

I'm not sure why Jerry took such an interest in helping me get started and I might not ever know. As nice as Jerry was, I never got as close to him as I did later with some of the other guys. He kept a little distant, like a teacher with a student, while the other deejays would become my friends. By the end of my first summer, Jerry got another job out of town and left WWCO forever. I can't remember what station he went to and I never saw him again, but about five years after he had moved on, I heard one of his tapes. It was his aircheck, what you send out to radio stations to show how you sound on your show, when you're looking for a new gig. It was in 1974 and Jerry was hoping to get his old job back at C-O. The program director at the station knew I used to

work for Jerry, so he let me listen to the tape. I wish I had never heard it. It was upsetting. I don't know if it was just because I was older, or because Jerry had changed, but it sounded like he was doing a parody of his old show, trying to revive his "pumpin" and "rappin" routine. His head was in a different space and his heart wasn't in it. What he once did so naturally and seemingly without effort, he was now trying to force it to get a job. It didn't work. I was uncomfortable listening to him as he spoke to the program director in what was an audio letter, asking him for a break. I was too young to know how to handle those feelings, too shaken to find out what happened to him.

I prefer to think of Jerry the way he looked and sounded the first time I met him, when he was the top deejay in town, the coolest guy on the radio. I realized for all the afternoons I spent with him that summer of 1969, I didn't even know if Jerry Wolf was his real name or something he made up. I just know without him, I might never have made it into radio. He was my teacher, mentor, the image of what I thought every disc jockey should be. Especially me.

The Sunny Side

I discovered my passion for radio at a relatively young age. It actually happened way before I met Jerry Wolf at WWCO. I was nine years old, when my fourth-grade class went on a field trip to the WTIC television and radio stations in Hartford. I was fascinated by the cameras and the lights in the TV studio but it was the on-air personalities of the two deejays that really got my attention. When our class stopped in front of their studio to watch them work, I found myself hanging on every word. Those guys were cracking jokes, playing music, while also waving at us kids through the glass window in front of their audio booth. I couldn't take my eyes off of them and nobody else in my class could either. Especially the girls.

Up until that very moment, I always thought work was, well work, like what my dad did at the factory. This was totally different. This was fun. In school I was never much of a student, but I was a talker and I knew how to make people laugh. Now here I was, standing right in front of two guys who were getting paid to talk and tell jokes on the radio. I thought, where do I sign up for THIS? How do I get in THAT room? It was a pivotal moment for me.

Being that young I didn't think too far ahead. It never occurred to me that I might not be able to make it in radio. When you're older, maybe you have a dream, or there could be something different you want to try, but then your mind starts to

work against you. Most people get stuck wondering how they're going to make it happen. What if this goes wrong, or what about that? But when you're young, you just do it. I learned early in life that you've got to go after your dreams, make your own luck, which is something I witnessed firsthand from my family, a bunch of hard-working, fun-loving, boisterous Italians.

My grandparents were from the Abruzzo region of Italy, about 75 miles east of Rome. They were farmers and like so many others, they sailed to America in the early nineteen hundreds looking for a better way to live. My dad's family made their home in the country where they had a small farm and my grandfather found work as a janitor. My mom's parents lived in the city. Lucky for me, both families ended up in Connecticut.

I grew up on the sunny side of life, on a street called Sunnyside Avenue. That name kind of says it all. I think my parents expected to have a big family with lots of kids, like how they grew up, and when that didn't happen, they were grateful to have Henry Junior and me, David Joseph. We were born nine years apart so I might have been called an accident or a surprise, but my mom called me a blessing. My big brother Hank may not have always felt so blessed. In many ways, Hank was like a second father to me, playing catch with me after school, helping me with homework, taking me in his car for ice cream at the local Carvel, basically keeping an eye on me. He was the smart one, a future college professor who was so good to me and I was, in return, so bad to him. Bad might be too extreme, I was mischievous. I came up with all sorts of creative ways to torture my big brother, in a loving way, of course. Like the time he showed me how to light a firecracker.

As a future teacher, Henry went through an impressive tutorial on how to hold, light, then toss a firecracker. It was so well presented, almost like one of those filmstrips you'd see in high

school with the announcer saying, "Firstly, grasp the firecracker firmly in your right hand." Actually, that was the problem. Henry is right-handed and I'm a lefty. When it was my turn, he lit the firecracker, then put it between two fingers in my right hand. With the fuse sizzling and proudly looking down, smiling at his student, he said, "Throw it!" I had never thrown anything with my right hand before. The longer I hesitated, the shorter the fuse got and the more agitated he got, until he yelled, "Throw it, you idiot!" So I did, awkwardly, and accidentally hit Henry in his forehead. The firecracker exploded and knocked his eyeglasses clear off his face, leaving a smudge of gunpowder just below his hairline. When his initial shock wore off and he reached down to gather up his glasses from the ground, I took off before he could put them back in place, knowing he would be in hot pursuit in seconds flat. But, come on, it was an innocent mistake, right?

Then there were all those times when I secretly tape-recorded his conversations with his girlfriend, my future sister-in-law Eileen. My mom and dad would be off on bowling night or out to dinner with friends. I waited until Hank and Eileen were downstairs in the living room, whispering and giggling together on the couch, then I quietly lowered a microphone down the stairwell. Probably the only time I ever did anything quietly. I'd listen in with headphones on, taping everything they said, then surprise them by playing back their most embarrassing moments. I knew there would be retribution, but it was worth it. Hank usually grabbed me around the neck to give me a major noogie on the noggin, one of many he handed out. I think I hold the record in Connecticut for being on the receiving end of the most noogies, ever. Sometimes my brother would change it up and just swat the back of my head. But Mom always came to my defense. She would yell out to Henry, "Stop hitting your brother in the head, you'll make him stupid." Thanks, Mom. Years later when I started working in radio, I told Henry how helpful it had

been to spy on him and Eileen. Learning how to use that tape machine turned out to be early training for my career behind the microphone. It seemed I had a knack for using that kind of equipment, something I picked up from my dad.

In my eyes, Henry Cipriano Senior could do just about anything. He was an inventor, a three-dimensional thinker. You could give him any kind of a project to work on and he would figure out how to get it done. We never hired a plumber, an electrician, or a contractor. My dad called himself "a Jack of all trades, master of none." He started each and every job the same way. The first thing he did was light up a Connecticut cigar, either a Muniemaker or an Evermore, then he sat down to think. It might take one hour, it might take three hours, but at some point during that process, when he was finished with his cigar, he knew exactly how to tackle that job, verbally explaining the blueprint he had drawn in his head.

Dad taught me how to do electrical work, wallpapering, fence building, bricklaying, how to finish off a basement, and many years later, when I moved to Los Angeles, he helped me build my first recording studio from the ground up. He was a successful amateur boxer in Waterbury, played baseball for the Oakville Townies, and after he discovered golf, he won the club championship several times over. Dad was introduced to his much-loved Connecticut cigars as a teenager, when he was hired as a picker in the local tobacco fields. As an adult, Dad worked for one company his entire life, the Scovill Manufacturing Plant. Everybody called it the Pin Shop because they made straight pins, safety pins, even the pins that hold together grenades. He never finished high school but that didn't stop my dad from becoming foreman at the Pin Shop. Dad was proud of his accomplishments without ever bragging. Coming from a very humble background, he was a wonderful success story.

Both of my parents lived through the Great Depression that started in 1929 but it hit my mom, Ermina Dantino, much harder. She grew up on the south side of Waterbury. Her dad had trouble finding a job so he worked the funeral circuit. The story goes, whenever there was a wake for someone who had just passed away, my grandfather was hired to wail and cry, even throw himself on the coffin, to prove how much the dearly departed had been loved by friends and neighbors. After all that effort he was paid one dollar for each appearance. Look at that, my first relative in show business. The problem was, he needed to make more money. If he brought another person to the wake, he could take home another dollar, so he recruited someone else to help out. My mom was eight years old when he started taking her to those funerals. Never mind that she didn't know anyone in the room, she definitely did not want to look at a dead body. Most times her tears came easily.

With money scarce, there were too many nights when Mom went to bed with an empty stomach, dreaming of cakes and cookies. There were days when the only food she had to eat was a piece of stale bread with a little sugar on top.

My mom was 11 years old when her dad died and the kids had to go to work to help support the family. Mom had just finished fifth grade when she quit school for good. She found a job as a maid for a lawyer and his family on the east side of town. Mom earned five dollars a week and bus fare was ten cents a day, so to save money she walked back and forth to work instead of taking the bus. It took her one hour each way. Mom worked for that family until she was 16 years old, when she got a job at a factory, the Peter Paul Candy Company in Naugatuck. She worked on the assembly line, just like in that episode of "I Love Lucy," where the candy rolls down the conveyer belt, as Mom and her best friend Faye Marinelli wrapped each piece and stuffed it into a box. When they introduced themselves and Faye heard Mom's

name was Ermina, Faye said, "Hell, I'll never remember that. I'll just call you Pat," and it stuck. From that moment on, even Mom called herself Pat, so did my dad. I don't know of anyone who ever called her Ermina. It was a very similar circumstance when many years later her son, me, would have his name changed from Dave to Joe just as quickly.

As hard a life as my mom had, she never dwelled on her difficult memories. Mom was tiny, not even five feet tall, tough, and also as sweet as can be. She would do anything for anyone without a word of complaint. She was deeply religious, saying her rosary twice a day as she sat on the edge of her bed. She never said an unkind word about anyone. My mom was a saint.

About one year after Mom met Faye, they were at a birthday party with a bunch of other people when this guy came up to Mom, took off his hat and put it on her head. That was my dad, flirting with a pretty young girl. They dated for one year and got married on October 28, 1939. My parents decided to move to the country where they could grow their own vegetables and have a few chickens. My mom would never go hungry again. Years later, even when they didn't have to worry about things like that anymore, my mom still agonized about wasting food. If our bread went stale before we finished it, Mom always gave the package a kiss and said a silent prayer before gently placing it in the trash. She knew what real hunger felt like. That's probably why Mom was always trying to feed everybody.

Every Sunday afternoon, all of my relatives would get together for dinner, usually at my parents' house. That meant anywhere from 40 to 50 people, aunts, uncles, cousins, all crammed into our small home, spilling out onto the yard to play bocce or baseball. As a young boy, I remember wandering from room to room, surrounded by deep, powerful voices all straining to be heard. Some of my aunts and uncles spoke Italian, others English, plus

there was a kind of a slang that mixed the two languages together. If I closed my eyes it sounded like a big orchestra warming up, all different instruments colliding and clashing until they came together for a lively musical production.

The show would open with a joyful melody as we greeted one another at the door with loud kisses on both cheeks. My uncles would tussle the hair on top of my head and my aunts would plant a red-lipsticked smacker on my face. That was followed by a good 30 or 40 minutes of friendly conversation, slowly building louder as more people arrived. Soon voices would be mingled with the clatter of plates, glasses, and silverware as everyone started to eat and drink. Then without fail, sometime between the main course and dessert, the music turned sharp when one of my uncles, accidentally or intentionally, insulted someone else. That brought on the battle scene, with all sorts of shouting and pointing and yelling, men and women, until I thought our house would explode. In the middle of that crazy commotion, at the height of hostilities, someone would break through the riot with a mention of their dear, dead mother, my grandmother, bringing everything to a screeching halt. What followed was deafening silence that could only be broken by one word…Mama! Only it came out as a slow, mournful, wail, "Maaaaa-Ma, Maaaaa-Ma." Then everyone started crying, tears flowed, a chorus of apologies filled the air, and peace was finally restored. That meant it was time for dessert. The day ended as it began, with warm hugs and kisses at the door and a promise to see one another next Sunday when we would do it all over again.

I had a front-row seat to my own private opera. I quickly learned if I wanted to be heard, I had to speak up. Loudly. I also learned how important family was to my mom and dad. No matter what was said during those raucous Sunday afternoons, at the end of the day, all was forgiven.

My parents didn't have a lot of money, but when the relatives came over for dinner, they knew they would be treated to a feast. It wasn't extravagant, but it was delicious. Mom started prepping the day before. There was homemade pasta, huge raviolis, cavatelli, and manicotti with her fresh tomato sauce, peppers, zucchini, and squash from the garden. In good weather Dad would cook outside on the grill, hamburgers and hot dogs. If it was a holiday, there would be turkey, ham, fish, you name it, we ate it. And then there were the pies. Mom was geared up for volume, making three or four pies every weekend. Cherry and apple were my favorite, then pumpkin, blueberry, and pecan. Everybody came for Mom's dessert and they would eat those pies all day long.

My dad wasn't a big drinker but as he liked to say, "Hey, I'll have a slug of that." It was usually beer, sometimes red wine, then he'd pass it to someone else and say, "Have a slug!" The thing was, if you wanted to be part any of the games they were playing, you most likely had a drink in your hand.

You haven't seen anything until you've seen a bunch of Italian men playing Morra. All my life I thought it was called Ahmode, but that was just the mixed-up Italian/English slang my relatives used to speak. It's a hand game between two people, kind of like rock, paper, scissors. Using one hand, you throw out any number of fingers you want to play, from zero to five. At the same time, you guess out loud how many fingers both of you will show together, from zero, on up to ten. For this game my uncles always counted in Italian, niente to dieci. And they didn't just shake their hand and toss out a few fingers. They used their entire body, rocking back and forth, then thrusting their arm out to flash a couple of fingers. And they didn't just call out a number, either. They shouted it out, loud enough for the entire block to hear. I loved the sound of my relatives yelling in Italian, "DUE! CINQUE!!! OTTO!!! TRE!!!"

It was fun hearing those different words coming out of those familiar deep baritones. The longer they played, the more boisterous they got. If you won, you had a drink. If you lost, you had a drink. If it was a draw, everybody had a drink. Basically the game was an excuse to drink and be loud and if a fight broke out in the middle, that was okay too because at the heart of it, the game was all for fun.

Other times there were party nights at our house, when my parents had their friends over to play cards. There was always music blaring out of our big console stereo, Frank Sinatra, Dean Martin, Perry Como, every great singer with an Italian last name. The men wore nice suits with ties, the women were in dresses, stockings, and high heels, with their hair done up at the beauty parlor. I would sit at the top of the steps of our two-story home, listening to them talk, all night. I especially liked it when one of the men brought his accordion along. From the opening note, everybody danced, including my mom and dad. There might be 20 people doing some sort of an Italian conga line in our living room. At some point in the evening, the guy would always play the "Tarantella," an old Italian folk dance, and everybody clapped along. Couples linked arms, they would swing one another around in a circle until they collapsed, exhausted at the end of the song. For me, it was another beautiful opera played out right before my eyes and ears.

My parents loved sharing their home, their food, their laughter with all of their friends and family. My dad worked hard his whole life and got the greatest joy out of the simplest pleasures, a slow sip of wine, a puff on his beloved cigar, taking care of his family. Sunnyside Avenue is the place where I hold most of my childhood memories. Hank endlessly pitched me a baseball in the backyard. Dad took a catnap every afternoon on the living room floor with his head propped up on the first step of the stairs. It

sure looked uncomfortable to me but he slept like a baby. When I misbehaved, Mom chased me up those same stairs with a wooden spoon in her hand, threatening to "sit on me" if she caught me. She weighed about 100 pounds. Even if she did sit on me, I don't think I would have noticed.

The house on Sunnyside Avenue is where I lived when I went on that field trip in fourth grade and discovered the wonderful world of broadcasting. That night, when I went to bed I tucked a transistor radio under my pillow so I could hear what the deejays said after dark. That was my first class in a crash course about rock and roll radio. It was the land of imagination. I couldn't exactly touch it, but I could feel it, and I knew I wanted to be a part of it. My journey was just beginning.

TOM COLLINS

In the neighborhood where I grew up, when school let out at the end of the year, no one went to summer camp. I had never even heard of camp. We played ball in the backyard, hung out at the mall, went fishing at Slade's Pond, rode our bikes all over Oakville, and watched the Red Sox and the Yankees play baseball on TV. After meeting Jerry Wolf and seeing the inside of a radio studio, I had something new to add to the list of activities during my summer vacation. I wanted to learn all I could about radio.

I started listening to every single station I could find. Late at night, I discovered that just by turning the dial, I could tune in AM frequencies from clear across the country. It was like a magic box had opened up just for me.

In those days, most AM radio stations had to lower their power at sundown, or go off the air entirely, until sunrise the next day. It was a rule made by the Federal Communications Commission. Imagine if you had 30 flashlights, beaming different colored lights from one end of a room to the other side. They would cross over one another, muting all the colors, getting in the way of each other. Then imagine turning all of them off except for two or three. That would open up a wide, unobstructed path of clear light to make it through to the other side of the room.

Even though AM radio doesn't broadcast in a straight line like that, it helps to visualize how I was able to listen to radio stations thousands of miles away from my home. After sunset, when the smaller stations shut down or lowered their power, the bigger clear-channel stations took over the airwaves. Instead of dozens of signals crowding the airways, now there were just a handful and they came in loud and strong. It seemed like some sort of trick and in a way it was. It even had a name. It was called "skipping." That's when those powerhouse monster AM's would slide in, their signals bouncing off the ionosphere, floating across the air, through my bedroom window, into my transistor radio under my pillow.

All at once a treasure chest of legendary stations opened up to me. That was way before computers, the Internet, or satellite radio. My dad had only just bought our first color TV. Being able to eavesdrop on those stations was like listening in to my parents' parties. I heard the big sound of Super CFL, the Voice of Labor, from Chicago, and WOWO, from Fort Wayne, Indiana. There was Detroit's CKLW, all the way from Windsor, Ontario, Canada, the sound of Boss Radio, the Big 8. Listening to those faraway voices, I thought the most exciting job anyone could have would be to work at a radio station. And to work at one of those stations in a big city would be my dream come true.

That picture in my mind is what kept me from going crazy when school started up in September of 1969. With classes about to begin again I knew I wouldn't be able to spend as much time at C-O as I wanted to, anymore. I had to make other plans, find some other way to continue my independent education. If I couldn't go to the station anymore, I figured I had to bring the station to me. So I built my own studio at home.

First, I bought a little audio mixer, a microphone and tiny

AM transmitter with less power than a walkie-talkie, all from a catalog called Lafayette Electronics. Then I found a couple of plastic turntables from Radio Shack for $10 each. I already had my own record case packed with forty-fives and I had a tape recorder I could use to play the jingles from WWCO. I even made copies of the commercials.

I picked up a piece of plywood and cut out a hole so the audio mixer knobs could stick through it, just like at the radio station. Only mine was held together with duct tape. It fit perfectly on the desk in my bedroom. But I didn't want to be the only deejay on my station, so I dragged two of my friends into it with me.

Most every day after school we went on the air for three hours. We called ourselves 1600 WOLF Radio. Somehow it just seemed right that the call letters should honor the guy who gave me my first break, Jerry Wolf. I did the first shift from four to five p.m., then my cousin Pete Simons did the second shift while I had dinner downstairs. My buddy Bill Lombardi rounded out our big-time staff from six to seven at night. I would be sitting at the kitchen table with my mom and dad listening to WOLF on our trusty radio on top of the fridge. It was the first time ever we turned the dial away from AM 1240 to a new frequency. We were rappin' and pumpin' out tunes, blasting our music out of that tiny 100-milliwatt AM transmitter. You could actually hear it halfway down the block in my neighborhood. I treated it like the real thing and even made airchecks of myself so I could listen to them later. It was my first on-air radio gig and I took it seriously.

It was also the first time I tried out a new name for myself. I didn't think anybody used his or her real name on the air,

and I had been looking around for months for something that sounded right. The most famous deejays were Cousin Brucie, Dan Ingram at WABC in New York and of course Jerry Wolf. I wanted a name that made me feel like a star. I scoured baseball rosters, TV shows, and the comics. I even picked up books from English class without being asked, something I would never have done before on my own. And then I found it, staring up at me out of the newspaper in, of all places, the obituary section. I was reborn, Thomas Collins. Only I would call myself Tom or even Tommy. I thought it was perfect. Tom Collins, yeah that works.

I still tried to get over to C-O whenever I could on the weekends. I was restless to get back to my real purpose in life, rock and roll radio. By the time summer finally rolled around again, we were deep into the beginning of a new decade, 1970, and on my first day of vacation I burst through the door of 65 Bank Street with big plans. I ended up hanging out at the station nearly every single night plus every weekend. My parents supported me all the way. I don't know if they were relieved I found something I could actually do for a living or if they were simply as fascinated by the whole thing as I was. I just know they trusted me.

I was still too young to drive so around five in the afternoon I was back at The Mighty Oak waiting for the bus to take me to C-O, then late at night, my dad drove downtown to pick me up. I guess it was one way to keep an eye on me. Most days, my dad worked from seven in the morning until three in the afternoon, but there he was, at eleven at night, puffing on his cigar, sitting in his car, listening to WWCO, waiting to drive me home from the radio station. I was a very lucky kid.

The previous summer at C-O, I was still a little star struck, seeing it all up close for the first time, getting my hands on the equipment. Building my own radio station at home gave me the confidence to keep going. It made me feel as if I really had a shot at making my dream come true. Now it was my second summer at C-O, time to show the guys what I could do. I ended up spending more time at Bank Street than many of the people who got paid to work there.

That was the summer I got to know all of the other deejays. Most of the guys were in their twenties and started working in radio right out of high school. A few had gone to college and one had served in the Army. They became a band of brothers, best friends connected by their love of radio. For some of them, WWCO would turn out to be the most fun working they would ever have, past, present, and future. In the late sixties, early seventies there were very few women on the air and C-O was definitely a boys' club. Tim Clark, Ron Gregory, and Mike Holland in particular were the greatest guys I could ever hope to know. There were plenty of others who came and went, Pete Moss, Jim Scott, Dick Springfield, Bill Raymond, Joe Sherwood. Each one had his own style and each one shared his wisdom with me. It was a kindness I've never forgotten.

But out of everyone I ran into at WWCO, I had never met a guy like Mike. I actually heard about him way before we were introduced. Mike was the first person I knew of who had gone to war. He had been working at C-O when he was drafted and ended up serving two years in Vietnam. Jerry Wolf used to send him reel-to-reel tapes, an audio letter, when Mike was still in the Army. On those days I helped out at the station, I watched

Jerry put his tapes together and often wondered what that guy Mike would be like if I ever got the chance to meet him. And then I did.

65 BANK STREET

The first time I saw Mike Holland, he was just back from the Vietnam War, hunkered down on his haunches on the floor of the AM studio, eating a sandwich. In my young mind I could picture him sitting just like that in some rice paddy in Southeast Asia. It was a sobering thought. I could only imagine what his experience there had been like in the war. I figured he was lucky to be alive, and always felt that he was hellbent on making up for lost time.

His real name is Michael Bouyea, but on the radio he was Michael Emerson Holland or M.E.H. as he sometimes called himself. Mike was on the air from six to ten at night at WWCO when he was drafted. I give a lot of credit to Wally King, our station manager, for rehiring Mike when he returned. By 1970, the Vietnam War was so hated throughout much of the country that soldiers were spit on when they came back home. It was nothing like today where we try our best to honor the men and women who serve in the military. Our boss did the right thing giving Mike back his job and whenever he needed time off from work for a little rest and rehabilitation, he got it, no questions asked.

I spent a lot of time with Mike that summer. Ever since Jerry

left, I wasn't sure where I would fit in so it was nice when I casually slipped into a routine with Mike. He seemed to like having me around. On warm nights, when his shift was over, we used to go out on the fire escape down the hall from the studio. He'd light up a cigarette and I would listen to him talk about radio. I was too timid to ask him about Vietnam. I didn't think it was my place to pry into that part of his life. Besides, I was already uncomfortably suspended in the air, six stories above the street. I liked the easy conversation of topics I understood better. We talked about school, music, and where we both wanted to work in the future. On nights he felt like blowing off steam, we raided the music library where all the old and now unused seventy-eight rpm records were kept, took them out on the fire escape, then sent them flying across the street to the roof next door, like a Frisbee. Unfortunately for anyone down below, not all of them made it. Fortunately for me, none of them hit my dad's car.

Sometimes I think of Mike as the devil on my shoulder, tempting me to grow up a little faster than I was ready. He was a man who had seen things I couldn't imagine, and I was a naive, small-town teenage boy. I definitely respected and admired him, because of his past. In the future, Mike would end up with one of the best careers in radio out of all of us at C-O. Back then, I was his willing wingman. Get this: as it turns out, being a deejay is a great way to meet girls.

It was like there was a magnet, pulling women across town, over to 65 Bank Street. I remember Mike, especially, had a parade of girls coming into the studio most nights. Some of those women were not exactly the type of girl you'd take home to mother. In fact, I don't think even their own mothers were thrilled about having these girls around. Once the office staff had gone home for the day, the groupies

started coming in. The evening's events usually began around eight o'clock. The elevator buzzer would go off and Mike would send me down to the first floor to bring up the girls. I'd get to the lobby, open the door and there right in front of me would be one or two girls, about 20 or 22 years old, smiling at me, their lips covered in bright pink lipstick. They'd ask how old I was and I always told them my real age, 15, but next to them I felt ten years old. I tried to act cool like Mike and say something funny, but honestly I had no idea what the hell I was doing. While I was bringing the girls up the elevator, Mike had run over to the jock lounge, grabbed a couple of those green vinyl cushions off the sofa and thrown them onto the floor in the bathroom. It had taken me one full year but now I knew where the stains came from on those cushions. Mike would meet us at the elevator, take hold of the girls, and then the greatest thing in the world would happen. But I don't mean what you're probably thinking. As they disappeared down the hallway, to do whatever they were going to do, Mike would hand over control of the station to me.

I was in heaven. I cranked up the music to ear-splitting levels in the control room and when that first record ended I would jingle into the next song. Wow, what a thrill. Before he went into the bathroom Mike told me, "OK, Davey, I'm gonna be in the back with this chick for about three songs. You need to do a song to song and then a song to jingle to song while I'm gone." Good God, I was running the goddamn radio station. I'd call my friends from Watertown High School and tell them to listen to this next song as it ends and when you hear the jingle and the following song, that was ME doing that. Mike would come back into the studio after the second song to say that he needed to talk before the next record to give the illusion that he was still running the show. He would say to me, "Why don't you go in there with the girls while I talk up this record?"

"What? Uh, no no no, that's OK," I'd reply. My high school sexual experience was like mere training wheels compared to these two-wheelers Mike was riding For now, I would much rather play the music, please. He'd do his quick bit on the air, then head back to the bathroom for more fun.

If Mike was the devil on my shoulder, Tim Clark and Ron Gregory were more like angels. Okay, not exactly angels but they were definitely better influences on me than Mike. They reminded me a little bit of my own brother, Henry. They came over to my house a few times and even my mom liked Ron and Tim. Many years later they honored her memory when they came to her funeral on a cold January day.

Tim had started out as a DJ just like I had, coming down to the radio station at night when he was in high school, so he got a kick out of showing me the ropes and paying back the favor. Tim worked every Saturday night on the AM from seven to midnight while Ron did the exact same shift across the hall on the FM. Ron had gone to the Connecticut School of Broadcasting. After he graduated he got into his Dodge Dart and drove up and down Interstate 95, stopping at every radio station along the way, looking for a job. When he got to WWCO, he was hired for the overnight shift on the FM station, playing country music. Eventually he took over the night shift on the AM station, calling himself "The Night Owl."

Tim and Ron were best friends, both in their early twenties. I can't think of one without thinking of the other. But there was something more profound for me. Ron was black and Tim was white. Today it sounds silly to say this, but back then, that made a huge impression on me. There were so few African-American kids at my high school that I didn't have any black friends. Now

here was this great guy right in front of me, Ron Gregory, who just happened to be black and I'm hanging out with him all the time. It was an early lesson for me that skin color didn't matter. Tim and Ron both looked out for me and actually protected me from some of the stuff that went on at WWCO. The most unforgettable lesson I learned from Ron was about women.

Earlier that summer Ron had given me a warning. He said, "Listen, Davey, there are going to be all kinds of girls that want to bang you just because you're a disc jockey. And when that happens, here's what I want you to do." With the hint of a smile he walked over to the door in the jock lounge and said, "When your dick gets hard because of one of these girls…take it out of your pants and stick it in this door jamb and you slam this door shut as hard as you can." Then he burst out laughing. Ron had the greatest laugh and when he started up you couldn't help but join in, but I got the message loud and clear: DO NOT THINK WITH YOUR DICK! Mike, on the other hand, seemed very content to have his dick lead him in and out of every willing woman in Waterbury. Most of them were really nice girls who just happened to feel the tug of that magnet pulling them down to Bank Street. Many of them ended up on the bathroom floor, lying on those green cushions from the jock lounge with their legs spread up in the air.

Out of all the women who went up and down that elevator, the one I will never forget was the girl they called Tug Boat Rosie. The first time I met her it was after ten o'clock when the buzzer went off downstairs. I followed my routine, took the elevator down, opened the front door, and tried to come up with something clever to say. Standing there in front of me was a short, thin, blond girl 18 years old, kinda cute, with a nice smile. Until

she took out her teeth. All of them. Before then, the only person I had ever seen without teeth was my 70-year-old uncle. I didn't know what to say. I was shocked. I wasn't thinking about what terrible thing might have happened to her or what kind of life she was living. Most of the guys didn't care, either. I'll never name names, but there were quite a few deejays that got the smoothest blowjob they ever had from Tug Boat Rosie.

Yes, believe it or not, deejays do have groupies and sure, lots of the guys met women and had sex at the station so I was in just the right place to pick up some pointers. Besides, I still had Tim and Ron looking out for me, not only about girls, but everything else, too. Ever since they met my parents, they took it upon themselves to protect me.

As far as the station manager Wally King knew, I was only at WWCO on Saturday afternoons, helping out by filing records. In reality, I was there nearly every night, plus all day on the weekend. Wally was a great guy, but he wasn't so crazy about me hanging around his radio station. The sales manager, Bob Somerville, was even more of a problem. He was a real button-down guy who went by the book. Bob was so straight we used to joke that he slept in his suit. The problem was, both of them had a habit of stopping by the station unannounced. Sometimes they were just checking up on what was going on and other times, they had out-of-town visitors who wanted a tour. But most of the time, they wanted to see if there were any women in the studio. I understood that Bob, Wally, and the rest of the management team weren't bad guys, they were just protecting their business. There were rules set up by the Federal Communications Commission and regulations that had to be followed and they weren't going to let a bunch of crazy disc jockeys cause them to lose their license.

On many Saturday nights, whenever we heard the elevator bell ring out announcing that one of the managers had stopped by, Ron and Tim would turn to each other and say, "What are we gonna do with the kid?" To stay out of trouble, the guys had found a few places to hide me. One of them was in the broom closet. The closet only had a half door, oddly enough the top half, so the bottom was open. That meant I had to stand with my feet inside two buckets while I covered my body with mops and brooms so no one would see my legs or shoes below the bottom of the door. Once when I was in there, Bob walked right by me and I held my breath until he passed me on his way to the studio.

There were other times I hid under the turntables in the FM studio. The engineer had built a console with two large wooden boxes on either side of the deejay, and mounted on top of each one was a turntable. There was an access door in front so you could get underneath to fix anything that might go wrong. I always remember Ron being on the air on the FM at that time and he would tell me, "Okay, Davey, get in the box!" I was pretty small so I crawled inside and stayed there for 20 or 30 minutes until the coast was clear. As long as Bob wasn't in the studio with him, Ron talked to me while the records spun on the turntables above my head and gave me a play-by-play of what was happening. The last hiding place was the fire escape, my least favorite of all. I hunkered down, rain or shine, hot or cold to wait until it was safe to come back inside, which is probably why to this day, I still don't like looking over the edge of a building.

That's how I spent my second summer at WWCO, taking the bus to the station, with my dad picking me up at night. Once I turned 16, my parents bought me my own car, an old Rambler Classic with "three on the tree," a three-speed standard shift on

the steering column. When school started back up again I had a newfound freedom to go to the station whenever I wanted, without asking my dad to pick me up. Maybe that's why he bought me the car. All during my junior year in high school I drove myself back and forth to C-O to hang out with Mike, Ron, and Tim. By now I had been at WWCO for nearly two years, working in the production room, hiding from the bosses, all the time listening, learning, and doing whatever the guys would let me do, waiting for my own break into show business. And when that opportunity came, I barely had any time to think about it.

THE GOODNIGHTS

Springtime is the luckiest time of year for me, ever since I was offered my first shot to go on the air as a real deejay on a real radio station. I remember the exact date. It was April 25, 1971. Still in tenth grade, I was at home with my family on a Sunday afternoon. Like always, my mom had cooked up one of her big Italian dinners with pasta, lamb chops, potatoes, fish, veggies, and of course a couple of pies for dessert. I was all stretched out on the couch, recovering from our big meal, talking to my brother Henry, his wife Eileen, and my mom and dad, when the phone rang. It was Rick Shay on the line. He was the program director for the FM country station.

"Hey, Davey Cipriano, this is Rick Shay. Listen I'm really in a bind. Do you think you're ready to go on the air?"

"On the radio?"

He laughed, "Yeah, do you think you can do it? Hank Cee can't make it tonight and I can't find anybody and I just thought, you know, you've been around here since I don't know how long, that maybe you're ready to do it."

Hank Cee was much older than me, probably in his thirties. He was on the air from nine until midnight every Sunday night.

He also had his own successful country music band and lately they were booking gigs a couple of nights a week, including Sunday. He just couldn't do the weekend radio show anymore. His shift was only three hours long so I said, "Rick, yeah, I'm ready to do it. Yes, for sure!"

For the past two years, I had been wishing and waiting for that moment to happen. I wasn't the least bit nervous. I had been "playing" at radio for so long, it felt natural. Besides, I was going on the FM station and other than my family, I couldn't imagine anyone else would be listening. I only had one hour to get downtown. I parked my car out front, took the elevator up to the sixth floor and calmly walked into the studio. Bob Edmunds was on the air and he gave me a nod as he wrapped up his show, then stood up from his chair. I saw a stack of forty-fives next to the console and grinned. I was used to hiding under that turntable, not putting records on top of it. As Bob left the room, I sat down, adjusted the microphone, and said my first live disc jockey words:

"This is Tom Collins playing your favorite country songs on WWCO FM Radio. Here's something I hope you'll like."

With the mic turned off, I finished the sentence in my head, "Because I have no idea what the hell I'm playing and I hope you don't notice." It was true, I didn't know anything about country music. There wasn't even a format to follow. You just had a stack of records and a rack on the wall full of country albums and you played whatever you liked. I figured that one of those records had to be a hit. I played a few songs I'd never heard of by groups I didn't know, but I pretty much stuck to what was familiar to me: Credence Clearwater Revival, the Nitty Gritty Dirt Band and Crosby, Stills and Nash. I was smart enough to throw in a few

old classic country songs as well from the albums lining the wall. I don't remember making any terrible mistakes so I guess it went all right. Rick was listening and he called me on the hot line that night to say, "You're doing great, kid, and I like the name!"

Then he asked me the most improbable question, "How would you like to do this every Sunday night?"

I thought, "Wow, he must have really been in a bind to offer me this job!" But I also know if you stick around long enough and work hard to learn the ropes, somebody will take notice and give you a break. And that's how it happened for me.

I quickly became somewhat adept at country music. I had a little help from some very devoted listeners. Those country fans kindly educated me whenever I mangled a singer's name, or made some other glaring mistake. Like the time I wondered out loud on the air if Jim Reeves would have a new song coming out soon. My next phone call was from a very nice lady in New Britain, Connecticut, who told me Jim Reeves wasn't writing music anymore because he had died several years ago. Good to know, I thought. She wasn't angry or making fun, she just wanted to help out. Since then, I've done a lot of different radio formats and I know, in my heart, there is no fan like a country fan.

I was still a junior in high school, working on the FM every Sunday night when just before the summer of '71, the entire radio station moved to a new location out in the suburbs. It was a round, modern building, two stories high, on Straits Turnpike in Watertown. One day we were on the air downtown at 65 Bank Street, and the next day everyone showed up at the new place, called Commerce Campus. It was a big change. We went from

vintage hardwood floors to modern, bright carpet. I missed the layered paint on the walls, thick with the smell of cigarettes and greasy food. One had a past filled with colorful stories, the other seemed bland and unexciting. It was a little like going from the Isley Brothers to the Osmond Brothers. Even the green sofa was gone, replaced by a new orange one, unstained for the moment.

After we moved to Commerce Campus, WWCO became more popular than ever, with a new generation of disc jockeys taking to the airwaves. Over the past couple of years there had been quite a few staff changes on the AM station. That's just how it is in radio. Disc jockeys come and go all of the time. Sometimes it's because the station has a new owner who wants to bring in different talent, other times it's a new program director, or even a format change. Now and then the jock needs a change of scenery, or he's received an offer from out of town. Jerry Wolf had left more than one year ago. By now, Tim was gone too, and Ron had left for Washington, D.C. Mike was in Hartford at WDRC.

A bunch of new and talented guys had been hired to work on the AM station and I was about to become one of them. I was 16 years old, still playing country music Sunday night on the FM station when the program director on the AM side asked me to work the Saturday night shift playing Top 40 music. Finally, all my hard work paid off. I was going to be a Top 40 deejay. Unbelievable. I was on the AM Saturday and the FM on Sunday. Then it got even better. In a few short months, by the time school started up again, I was offered the job I set my heart on, so many years ago. I was finally going to go on the air, full time, on the most popular station in town.

It was the fall of 1971 when I became part of the family, a

member of that exclusive band of brothers playing the Top 40 hits on 1240 AM, WWCO. I had just turned 17 years old, a senior in high school, when that lone Saturday night shift I had been doing for the past six months turned into a full-time gig. I was on the air Monday through Friday, from six to ten every night, Mike Holland's old shift, doing my homework while the records were playing. All those years of soaking up Jerry Wolf's rappin' and pumpin' banter, running the elevator for Mike's late-night visitors, and hanging out with Tim and Ron had brought me to this moment. Now it was my turn, my time, to show off what I had learned.

This was one of my first experiences with the power of theater of the mind, where words and sounds create a reality all in your imagination using only one of your senses, the sense of hearing. I was inspired by the wit and style of two major disc jockeys, Don Imus at WNBC in New York and John Records Landecker at WLS in Chicago. Imus in the Morning was outrageous and cantankerous. When he put people on the air with him, they had better be ready for scornful remarks and rude hang-ups. Landecker was a true Top 40 jock and his station, 89 WLS, was one of those clear-channel stations that barreled into Connecticut late at night when I was a kid. He had it all, timing, humor, and a great comedy bit he called "Boogie Check." He put his listeners on the air just to talk, not for a contest, or to request a song, just to check their boogie, as he would say. I incorporated Imus' sarcastic tone with Landecker's humor and came up with something that was my own. Something I called "The Goodnights."

When I turned on that microphone I believed I was turning on the entire town of Waterbury to something new. I had come up with a funny bit that I thought was both innocent and spicy,

that would appeal to everyone. It started out as a cute idea to take a few phone calls live on the air from listeners, saying goodnight to me at the end of my shift. I wanted to include the listeners in the show, create an atmosphere of a party where all of us were in this together, enjoying the music and having fun on the radio. The end of the show "goodnights" grew into a nightly ritual that became longer and longer and more and more popular. It was a playful, testosterone-fueled romp through the budding female flowers of Waterbury. The ultimate prize for a caller was to be one of the girls who were put on "hold." So the girls that got through on the phone to say, "Goodnight, Tommy," had two things on their minds, to lie about their age and to try and to talk as sexy as possible. Everyone played their part perfectly and it was good radio theater.

The voice is a wonderful thing. You can manipulate it to paint a mental picture that is not always based in reality. In this case there were a lot of 16-year-old girls who had the rather impressive skill to "sound like" what the actress Farrah Fawcett "looked like." This made for some good radio and because I was a teenager too, it was all innocent. I wasn't a dirty old man preying on young teenage girls. I was a horny high school kid preying on young teenage girls my own age. Did I meet and date some of them? Oh yeah! But nowhere near the listener's imagination.

Every night on my show, girl after girl after girl would call in one after the other and I would act rather bored by their pussycat purring until they said something particularly titillating, whereupon I'd ask, "Excuse me, how old are you, honey?" Here I am at 17 years of age calling a girl "honey"! I was overextending the bounds of my own reality. If they said 14 or 15, I'd make a

rude comment such as "Call me back in a few years" or "Does your mother know you call ridiculously handsome disc jockeys late at night?" and then hang up on them.

Getting hung up on during the goodnights was just about as good as getting put on hold. But when a girl would say she was 18, my indifferent attitude would change to mock interest, "Really? So uh, tell me what do you look like, Tanya?" Or Heather or Brandy or whatever other name the caller had made up to make herself sound even sexier. They'd give an enticing description of what they looked like, including intimate body measurements, hair color, and their various state of undress, upon which every male hormone of every male listener would go into warp-speed overdrive. She might say, "Well, Tommy, I'm 5 foot 2 and blonde and my measurements are 36-24-36." I would let a beat go by, clear my throat, and say, "Hmm, why don't you hold on a minute here," and I'd hit the hold button that would give the most delicious comical sound effect on the air. The reverb of that hold button, clunk-clunk, meant Tom had a hot one on the line and then I'd quickly move on to the next caller.

As the weeks and months rolled by, the girls played along in the game and learned from past callers how to be even sexier and push it to the next level within the limits set by the Federal Communications Commission. The guys on the other hand would be driven to hormonal nirvana. It was better than paying for a Playboy Magazine because each guy listening conjured up a different image in his head of what each girl must look like and because it was all in their imagination, the image was ten times better than any Playboy Bunny. I would amp it up by having five or six girls on hold at one time and in between taking new calls I'd go

back to the girls on hold, remembering each and every one of their names for follow-ups. It was all comically timed to occur right after I unceremoniously hung up on a 15-year-old girl, slapping her with a snide remark, then I'd zip back to one of the girls on hold with an audible telephone clunk and whisper, "So, uh, Heather, you say you're blonde and you're 36-24-36, huh? So…ahem, what would a night with you be like, I mean if we had the opportunity to accidentally meet each other in a quiet place, such as the back seat of my car in the WWCO parking lot? Could you tell me…ahem, what would happen?" Then would come that beautiful AM radio phenomenon caused by "silence." The audio processing equipment at the transmitter would leap into Defcon One mode: dead air was happening!! The dead air would cause the audio compressors in the equipment rack to frantically seek out something, anything that was audible. The end result is similar to reaching over to your sound system and cranking the volume knob all the way up to ten. The equipment would search and lock in on the only sound it could find at that particular moment, the light breathing of a sensuous, theater-of-the-mind Christie Brinkley model look-alike, as her lips lightly touched the mouthpiece of her Princess telephone and she would purr in a whisper, "Anything you want, Tommy."

You could feel it, almost hear it. At that very moment at 9:59 p.m. and 50 seconds, as my on-air shift came to an end, all over Waterbury the sound of every teenage boy's head exploding and every girl giggling with the newfound knowledge of how to drive a boy absolutely crazy. As the clock on the studio wall clicked 9:59 and 52 seconds, 53 seconds, I'd pause and clear my throat and say, "Ahem…could you hold on a moment?" And then hit the button for the WWCO jingle, igniting the fuse which set off a mellifluous chorus of singers belting out, "Double-U, Double-U,

SEE OHHH" right into "Rock and Roll, Hoochie Koo," or some other Number 1 song on the chart that week, as I screamed over the top of the song intro, "Goodnight evrahbawdyyyy!"

The beauty of it was in the unknown and the perception of what just happened. Did Tom really meet that girl after the show? Oh my God, was she really that freaking gorgeous and did she really do "anything he wants?" Reality could never live up to the wild imagination of every listener out there. But it sure gave everyone a damn good reason to tune in tomorrow night to take this sexual ride all over again.

I was living my dream. From the top of that AM transmitter, for as far as the eye could see, I was a star. Beyond that, of course, I was a nobody. I lived in a bubble created by the magic of a small-town Top 40 radio station. I was completely intoxicated by that world of imagination. Dialing in stations from thousands of miles away, meeting other guys who were as excited to be on the air as I was, making friends and becoming part of a team, that was what it was like to be in the radio business back then. Most of us were young and a little bit stupid, but we sure had a good time. Kind of like misfits, in a fraternity of radio geeks. And I was just a kid, the youngest deejay at C-O, making mistakes, not knowing any better. The kind of guy who liked to push my limits.

Once when I was on the air, still working on the FM station, I suddenly had a craving for a roast beef sandwich from Arby's for dinner. The closest drive-thru was by the Naugatuck Valley Mall, ten minutes away without traffic. I considered the timing of it all, ten minutes there, five minutes to order and receive my dinner, ten minutes back to the station. If I put on an album that lasted a half an hour, I'd have five minutes to spare, no problem. "Tom

Collins here on WWCO FM and I thought I'd do an album spotlight tonight, playing an entire side of one album for you. Hope you enjoy it." I bolted out of the studio, jumped into my '72 Mustang and made it to Arby's no problem although there was a line to order. I hustled through that line and in no time I was on my way back to the station, when I realized the album was already on its last track. I drove like a maniac, sweating, frantic to get back to C-O, and I still had a five-minute commute left ahead of me. Then I heard the sound that no deejay, program director, station manager, or listener ever wants to hear on the air. The sound of silence. Actually it was more like "tsch, tsch, tsch," the sound of the needle bumping up against the label at the end of the album. I was devastated. When I hit the parking lot, I flew into the station and made up some ridiculous excuse for messing up on the air. That was the last roast beef sandwich I had in a long time.

In those early days on the air, I tried all kinds of tricks to get out of a jam. Those were the days when a small-town radio station had its own news and sports departments. The guys wrote up stories with taped interviews that we played throughout the day. Sometimes the reporters read their own copy, but at night they went home and it was up to the deejays to deliver the news. That was still during the Vietnam War and if you can remember, some of the names of those battlefields were hard to pronounce. On my shift, I had to "rip and read" from the wire service machines. That meant while a song played, I ran into the newsroom to rip the latest story off of the machine, then got ready to read it on the air during the news update. On my way back into the studio, I glanced at the copy from the wire machine and often realized I had no idea how to say some of the names of these Vietnamese

towns. Even if it was written out phonetically, I was still unsure. One night, I just panicked. In the middle of reading the story loaded with those unfamiliar words, I did what anyone would do, I reached over to the control rack and I killed the transmitter. I turned the entire radio station off the air. After ten seconds, I turned it back on, whereupon I said, "and that's news, now let's look at Waterbury weather…" as if nothing had happened.

As a deejay back then, we were always performing in real time, live to the audience, without any do-overs. Usually you're alone in a studio, with that built-in cloak of invisibility. But soon I started making personal appearances, along with the rest of the guys. It seemed we were constantly broadcasting from some remote location, county fair, car dealership, inside a bowling alley, the annual dance marathon, any place that wanted a little publicity, WWCO was there. When the city of Waterbury turned 300 years old, the station picked me to broadcast live from a hot-air balloon. I don't think anyone else volunteered and I could never say no. Standing in front of a live audience, there's no hiding behind the microphone. I found out how much I loved performing, facing that fear. I craved that kind of pressure. It was an unforgettable time of my life.

Even though it has its limitations, I will always love AM radio. Especially growing up on the air, in the sixties and seventies, I felt there was a pure beauty in the AM sound that will never be duplicated. For me it was a living, breathing signal that picked up my voice and took it to the heavens and back again. Along the way it grabbed energy out of thin air as the sound waves ricocheted off the ionosphere again and again, thousands of times in an instant before they hit my headphones. I discovered sounds

that would never exist on FM or satellite radio that gave the AM signal depth and texture. Static rattling my studio speakers was a sunspot exploding in space. That crackling murmur was the wind whispering in my ear. I could hear lightning strike from a storm miles and miles away before I ever saw the flash in the sky. It was exhilarating. It was alive. AM radio was like seeing the Beatles in person, performing at the Hollywood Bowl, it was loud, exciting, and raw. Almost too hot to touch. FM radio was like listening to an intimate acoustic performance in your living room, pure, pristine, and real. A sound you could feel and caress. Both were unique and both were defined by the generations they served.

But as Bob Dylan foreshadowed several years earlier in the title of his song, "The times, they are a changin.'"

Boys Club

I met some crazy characters while I learned how to be a deejay. You've already been introduced to the guys at 65 Bank Street, but I also worked at C-O's new location in the suburbs, called Commerce Campus, from 1971 until 1975. Three great years and one very long year when I thought I would never make it out of Connecticut. Now when I go back home to see my family, I always drive by that funny round building with the thin walls, and smile. It's a trip back in time, where I met a group of smart, talented, creative deejays who just happened to pass through our town on their way to the next big thing.

Bill Raymond was one of the few who made the move from 65 Bank Street to the new studio. Like me, he worked on the AM and the FM stations. There was this one night he was on the air when I dropped in to hang out like I usually did on the weekend. I must have annoyed Bill with hundreds of questions, because all at once, I turned around in time to see an album flying through the air, aimed straight at my head. I ducked at just the right moment. I think that was the last time I sat in the studio with Bill. It wasn't until years later, when we were catching up on the old days, that I found out he had been roommates with Jerry Wolf. He filled me in on a couple of unanswered questions. First of all, Jerry Wolf was

his real name. I always wondered about that. Also, he said Jerry was one of the nicest guys you would ever meet. Bill said, "Jerry had a heart of gold. Of all the guys you could have called on the air in 1969, he was the right one. You were very lucky." I knew he wasn't kidding. There were a few guys who told me to get lost when I first showed up at WWCO, but Jerry wasn't one of them. He was one of the good guys. Good thing I didn't call Bill.

There was another deejay at C-O who became one of my closest friends, a guy named Johnny Walker. I know, Tom Collins and Johnny Walker, brilliant, right? What can I say? We were young. He was 19 years old when he was hired at the station in 1972, around the time I graduated from high school. Finally I was catching up to everybody else, meeting guys my own age. I had barely been introduced to Johnny when he helped me out of a jam. My boss at that time was Tom Coffee, a big Irishman, kind of a blustery guy who liked to play it tough, but he was really a sweet guy. He's the guy who gave Ron Gregory his very first job in radio on the country station. He's also the guy who refused to give me the night off so I could go to my senior prom. He said, "If you wanna work in radio, you don't get any holidays." My prom was on a Friday night and it wasn't until Thursday afternoon that he finally said, "Alright, you can go. I'll get someone else to work your shift." Johnny turned out to be that someone else.

Johnny was about medium height with a full, fuzzy beard, nearly as round as he was tall. He had a great big grin to match his girth. I think Johnny nearly always had a smile on his face because Johnny was nearly always high. The police pulled him over once late one night with another close buddy who happened to be our newsman, Steve Martin. They were petrified, convinced they

were about to be arrested when one of the cops focused his flashlight on Johnny's face in the passenger seat of the car. The beam of light fanned out over Johnny's long beard, ample chest and stomach, highlighting all the burn holes in his polyester shirt from the hot seeds that had popped out of the joint he had been smoking. When the officer saw the pack of rolling papers sticking out of Johnny's front pocket, he fought hard to stop from laughing but it was too much. "What would it look like in the morning paper that the night disc jockey and newsman for WWCO were arrested for possession of marijuana?"

Steve knew all too well what would happen and he said, "It wouldn't be good."

The state cop said, "Damn right, but I like WWCO, I listen all the time." Surprisingly he let them go with a warning.

My friendship with Johnny and Steve made me face a dilemma I had been struggling with for months. It seemed that everyone I knew, especially at the radio station, was smoking pot. That is everyone but me. I have never smoked, snorted, or injected any kind of drug. I was around it constantly, it was a part of my life, but I just wasn't interested. I was beginning to think something was wrong with me for not wanting to try it, so I asked my big brother Henry what he thought.

"All the guys I know smoke pot and I've never done it, but they all love it and have so much fun doing it. Do you think I should try it? Would you ever do it?"

"Well," he said, "if I smoked pot and then I did something I was really proud of, or some sort of accomplishment, I would never know if it was me, or because I was high when I did it. And that would bother me."

As usual, Henry gave me an honest answer that cut right to the heart of everything what was most important to me. Some people take drugs to escape their lives and other people do it to intensify an experience. The truth was, for me, I didn't want to change anything. I didn't need to change anything. I loved every moment of my life at WWCO. It was my dream and the last thing I wanted to do was alter that reality. I was thrilled to be doing what I was doing with every day a new adventure. I was excited about my glamorous radio career. I have always been strong in my convictions, determined that if I set my mind on a particular goal, I would succeed. Some might call it arrogance. I call it confidence. I was nakedly ambitious with one thing in mind. I wanted to work at one of those powerhouse radio stations I used to listen to late at night. That was much more important to me than smoking pot, or trying something else. I never felt that I missed out on anything. Besides, by now you must have me figured out. I take risks when it comes to my job, but in my personal life, I'm more of a straight-arrow kind of guy. A guy who likes to have fun.

Johnny, Steve, and I used to cruise around town between our shifts, with me as the designated driver. Once they had had a few hits off a joint, I would take them to the top of a big hill in Oakville, then race back down, banging my foot on the floor of the car, shouting that the brakes were out. Johnny would grab onto the dashboard and scream his heart out, with Steve yelling just as loud in the back seat. They were usually so blasted, that stunt worked every time. Being the straight man I ended up entertaining those guys, putting on a one-man show to get them to laugh. Johnny called me "Kid." The little dude in the front seat, making all the goofy comments.

Now that I had graduated high school, that spring of 1972, WWCO had become my new home. I spent more time at Commerce Campus than I did at Sunnyside Avenue. I never even thought about applying to college because I was already working the job I most wanted in life. Even when I had finished my own shift, I would hang out with the deejay on the air, or meet up with the guys in the jock lounge. There were still plenty of girls who wanted to meet a deejay and we were happy to hang with them, too. Saturday night in particular was known as visitor's night, mostly because of Eddie Maglio, one of the salesmen at the station. Eddie loved doing live broadcasts from around town in support of local charities and on the weekend he had his own radio show. He called himself The Mad Hatter, and wore a leather top hat to all of his appearances. He probably raised hundreds of thousands of dollars for different charities at those events. Every Saturday night, at nine o'clock, he would kick off his show playing "Stairway to Heaven" by Led Zeppelin. When he was on the air, The Hatter always had a couple packs of Marlboro cigarettes lined up on the audio board, and one of those packs was full of joints. Whoever was around would meet up in the parking lot, with one of the guys going in to see The Hat to score a couple of joints. After a while The Hat would throw everyone out to go back on the air for something he called The Lover's Hour. It was kind of a sad, tearful show filled with songs about breaking up and making up, and you could always hear Eddie singing along in the background.

Dick Springfield was another deejay I will never forget. He helped me figure out when it was okay to push the limits or when it was better to play it safe. Dick was the morning man and music director at WWCO in our new Commerce Campus location.

He was tall, thin, and always doing eighteen things at once. He would frantically run into the studio and ask me, "Hey, Tom, have you heard this record? What do you think?" Most times, before I could answer, he would be out the door asking someone else the same question. Dick was a smart, funny, all-around nice guy and he went on to enjoy great success later in life as a radio consultant on the West Coast. Dick lived about three hours north of Los Angeles in San Luis Obispo and years later, in the 1990s, after I had moved to L.A., whenever he was in town, we would get together for lunch or just hang out for a while to catch up with one another. Sad to say, Dick passed away much too young and radio played a role in the story of his passing.

I'm going to jump ahead for a moment to tell this particular story. It happened in June of 1998. Dick was up north when he was admitted to the hospital for emergency heart surgery, a complication from dental work he had done years earlier. His wife, Bobbie, and their daughter were driving from San Luis to San Francisco to be with him after his surgery and during the drive they were listening to a Frisco station that Dick programmed. The song they were listening to started to fade out and, as usual, they waited for the disc jockey to jump in with something smart to say but that didn't happen this time. Instead the song continued to fade out much longer than normal and after a moment of silence, as the microphone was turned on, they heard some noise and confusion in the background. The disc jockey was a woman, and when she came back on the air she spoke with a heaviness in her voice. Tenderly, she told her audience that she had just gotten news of someone very dear to the station who had passed away after heart surgery. As Dick's wife and daughter entered the city that night, it was their car radio that brought them the news that

their beloved husband and father was gone. As much as it hurt to find out that way, Bobbie told me later that it was just so right to hear that heartbreaking news through the medium that Dick loved so much.

Back at C-O, before I knew it, another year passed. My determination at work had paid off and I was promoted to afternoon drive, on the air from two in the afternoon to six at night. I followed a guy who was different from any other deejay I had ever met. His name was T.J. Martin, a smooth-talking ladies' man, twice my age. We heard that T.J. had a wild affair with the woman who wrote the best-selling book "Peyton Place." She divorced her husband to marry T.J. but as much as T.J. loved her, he was much fonder of classic cars and handmade suits. Two years after they were married, when he had helped blow through all that Peyton Place money, T.J. stuffed the trunk of his 1964 Mustang with all his clothes, then took off in the dead of night. Somehow he ended up working at Commerce Campus, cooing to the local ladies of Waterbury.

T.J. was hired for the midday shift, ten in the morning till two in the afternoon, to charm and sweet-talk the housewives listening at home. I know it sounds sexist, but first of all, it was 1972. It was sexist. Secondly, it was Top 40 radio where every day-part is clearly identified. Six to ten a.m.? Wake up people, give them the news they need to start their day, and a heavy dose of fun and hit music. Ten a.m. to two p.m.? Kids are in school, not able to listen and people who worked were at their desks. In '72, nobody listened to the radio at work, it wasn't allowed. The only audience left out there was officially "housewives." Who do you put in that midday shift for that audience? Someone who can

make housewives forget their day-to-day chores, put a smile on their face, and help them fantasize a little. Enter T.J. Martin, Mister Cool. He oozed charm and sophistication and dressed the part too, wearing tailored sports jackets, pocket squares, Italian slacks, clothes his wife bought for him before he skipped out on her. Every day T.J. showed up at the station looking suave, immaculate, a little bit like the singer Dean Martin. He always brought his lunch with him and a thermos of coffee to sip on during his shift. But by the end of his show, he had lost some of that luster. He not only looked like the character Dean-o portrayed on TV, he sounded like him too. T.J. slurred his words, missed his cues, and talked over the lyrics of every song. Finally someone figured out it wasn't coffee in that thermos. It was vodka. By the end of his shift, T.J. was smashed.

Our general manager at that time was Bill Raymond, the same guy who threw the record at me. He wasn't going to take that shit from anyone. Bill sat down with T.J. to tell him he just couldn't drink on the air anymore, it had to stop, so T.J. promised to go cold turkey. Instead of bringing his thermos to work, he started bringing in fruit every day, apples, grapes, even a bag of oranges, to snack on during his shift. Only his show didn't get any better. Somehow, T.J. was still getting loaded by two in the afternoon. It took Bill a couple of weeks but he finally solved the mystery. Every morning, before he came to work, T.J. injected the grapes and oranges with his favorite drink of choice. You guessed it, vodka. Before they could fire him, T.J. skipped town in the middle of the night, just as he did when he left his wife. We heard all kinds of stories about him, that he faked his death, he changed his name, maybe he moved to Colorado, but we never found out what really happened.

Around the time T.J. disappeared was the same moment AM radio started to lose its grip as king of the airwaves. By 1974, the FM frequency that we all laughed at and dismissed back in the sixties would begin to reveal its true potential. Our FM country station was 20,000 watts, and covered hundreds of miles from Massachusetts, through the entire state of Connecticut, on down to Long Island. The AM signal was a paltry 1,000 watts and barely made it past Waterbury. At sundown the signal dropped to 250 watts, just a little bit stronger than the light bulbs in your home. You could just about toast a slice of bread with that power. WWCO-AM 1240 may have been state of the art for its time but its days were numbered, and closing in fast.

As FM was taking over, we were going under. When we should have been doing everything we could do to stay fresh and on top, we tightened up. Bill Raymond had moved on and we had a new program director who seemed out of touch with the reality around us. He called the station "The Famous 1240" and the deejays were now "The Good Guys." Instead of sounding like the cutting-edge station we had always been, we started sounding like something out of the nineteen fifties. C-O would make one last great comeback under the guidance of Joe McCoy with a group of talented deejays, but for now, I was desperate to leave. I was still doing the afternoon shift at C-O when I became the music director, which was Jerry Wolf's job when I first met him at the old studio on 65 Bank Street. I liked the added responsibility, but I was always angling for more.

I got lucky and picked up a part-time shift at my dream station, WDRC, in Hartford. Everybody called it The Big D and for me, it was my first little step towards the big time. Coverage of the

two stations overlapped, so I had to come up with another name to use on the air at "Big D." I was still Tom Collins at WWCO, but at WDRC I called myself Dave Donovan. I was inspired by Dan Donovan at WFIL in Philly, Dale Dorman at WRKO in Boston, and Dr. Don Rose at KFRC in San Francisco. I liked the alliteration of the two "D" names, it just sounded cool to me. Twenty years later, in 1994, I would meet the ultimate Mister Cool, another "Double D." I'll get to that story a little bit later.

But for now I was stuck. In the blink of an eye another year rolled by and it was New Year's of 1975. My life was at a standstill. Johnny Walker had recently left for Q105-FM in Tampa, Florida. Steve Martin was gone too, now the morning newsman at WRVQ-FM in Richmond, Virginia. And I was still at WWCO-AM, doing everything I could to move up and out of my hometown but truth be told, as my friends moved on, I was left behind.

EVERYBODY'S MAKING IT BUT ME

As the music director of WWCO I received boxes of records every week from the record companies, with each song promising to be the next big hit. One day there was a song that landed on my desk that put a lump in my throat. It was actually a country tune by Shel Silverstein and the title summed up my feelings at that time. It was called "Everybody's Makin' It But Me." I tacked it up on my wall as a grim reminder of where my head was. I had been at WWCO for six years now, since I was 14 years old. I was making one hundred and fifty dollars per week. I sent out airchecks all up and down the East Coast, trying to move my career forward, but nothing was happening.

I had somewhat absentmindedly sent my tape to WRC in Washington, D.C. At about the same time, I got a hit from another one of my tapes. A radio consultant named Mike Joseph was starting up a new station in Providence, Rhode Island, called WPJB. He asked me to come to town for an interview, and when I got there he offered me a job, but they wouldn't tell me what shift I would get. All they said was, that's the way Mike Joseph works. This was not at all normal. Usually you are hired for a specific shift on the air, but Joseph preferred to keep his new hires on edge. I wasn't sure I wanted to move to Providence, I had hoped to get to a bigger city, but I wanted out so badly that I

accepted the job. It would be several weeks before the station was up and running, so I kept working at C-O and the Big D, killing time, till I packed my bags for Providence. Then I got a call from Washington, D.C.

"Hello, Tom? This is Gordon Peil, program director at WRC Radio in Washington. We like the tape you sent us but we're looking for deejays that can perform in a personality format with fewer restrictions than Top 40. Do you have anything else you can send us?"

"Yeah, sure. I've got a tape from another station I work at up here and I'll send it right away."

I sent him a Dave Donovan tape from WDRC, which was more of a free-form, personality-heavy station. One week later I was on the air at C-O when I got another call from Washington.

"Hello, Tom? This is Gordon Peil, program director at WRC Radio in Washington. As you know, we like the tape you sent us and we've narrowed our search down to three people and you're one of them. We're still sorting out things here but we would like to have you come down for an interview in a few weeks."

I hung up the phone and I was still in a daze when I got a call from one of the secretaries at WDRC in Hartford.

"Dave? I've got a message here for you from Gordon Peil in Washington. He wants you to call him back right away."

If this sounds confusing to you, imagine the state I was in at that moment. I was live, on the radio, doing my afternoon show. I just found out I had a one in three shot at a job in the number eight market in the country, and for some reason they've called me again up at WDRC. I called him back right away.

"Hi Gordon, you left a message for me at WDRC in Hartford…"

"Yes of course, WDRC. You must be Dave Donovan, right? This is Gordon Peil, in Washington. I want you to know that you are one of three candidates we're looking at for the opening at WRC."

"Wait a minute," I said. "I just talked to you about a half hour ago."

"No, we haven't talked to you before, Dave."

"Well, yeah, you called me here at WWCO where I'm Tom Collins."

"You're Dave and Tom? You're both the same person?" he asked. "Well then, whoever you are, it looks like you are two of the three people we're considering for this job. How soon can you get down here for an interview?"

"Right away!"

I never knew who the third deejay was, but I do know there were discussions that turned into arguments about who was the better candidate, Dave Donovan or Tom Collins, before the folks at WRC knew we were the same person. That next week they flew me down to DC. I was 20 years old and yes, I'm a small-town guy, so it was my very first time on an airplane. It was surreal.

I landed at Washington National Airport where there was a car waiting to take me to 4001 Nebraska Avenue, the home base of NBC in Washington. That's where WRC was located. I had never seen anything like it. It was a sprawling complex on more than seven acres in Northwest D.C. When I walked into the lobby there was a picture on the wall of David Brinkley, one of the most famous newsmen in the world. The hallways were noisy with people scrambling back and forth, everybody looked important, everyone was in a hurry, including cameramen who

lugged equipment over their shoulders as they hustled to their news cars in front of the building. It took me back to that first time I walked off the elevator at 65 Bank Street, when I realized my life was about to change forever. I felt that exact same thrill as I walked off the elevator at NBC.

I had a big smile on my face when I thrust out my hand to meet Gordon Peil. He looked just like what I expected a corporate executive to look like at NBC. He had trim brown hair, wire-rimmed eyeglasses, and he wore a brown suit with a brown tie. His office was pristine, with papers neatly stacked on his desk, and airchecks from disc jockeys were alphabetized on a shelf against the wall. Standing next to him was one of the tallest men I have ever met in my life, a radio consultant from New York, Bob Henabery. He was completely different from Gordon. Well over six feet, six inches tall, Bob had stark white hair and a full beard to match. He sometimes hesitated when he talked and emphasized every thought. We later nicknamed him the Great White Rabbit, in honor of the invisible rabbit in the Jimmy Stewart movie, "Harvey." (Look it up, it's a classic.) Looking at these two very different men somehow put me at ease. If they could work together, why not me? I was relaxed and my interview seemed to go well. It was easy and fun and they told me they would call soon to let me know the outcome.

Back home, I was walking on air. I couldn't wait to find out the verdict, but the Providence, Rhode Island, job that I accepted was getting close to being ready for my arrival. One morning before going into work at WWCO, the phone rang at my house. Both my dad and my mom were home. Mom answered the phone and called upstairs to me, "It's that Gordon guy from Washington." Holy crap. This is big. Will he say, "Sorry, kid, somehow we made a big mistake. There is no way NBC would ever consider a 20-year-old who lives with his parents in Oakville, Connecticut. But don't

worry, we take the responsibility for the error. There must be something terribly wrong with our system here in looking for new talent."

I picked up the upstairs hallway phone, then paused for a moment realizing it was the very same phone I used to call Jerry Wolf six years earlier.

"Hello?"

"Hi Tom or Dave or whatever your name is, Gordon Peil here from NBC in Washington."

"Yes, hi Gordon how are ya?"

"I'm good but not as good as you. I'll just cut to it. I wonder, Dave or Tom…would you be interested in coming to Washington to work with us?"

What the hell did he just say? "Uh, yes I would. Is this a trick question?"

Gordon laughed. "No of course not. Listen we loved your Tom Collins tape and when we heard your Dave Donovan tape we were over the moon. We really want you for our new station, would you consider it?"

"Yes, I would consider it. I mean yes!"

"Great, we'll send you some paperwork and give you two weeks to give notice at your current job. Sound good?"

Sound good? I had never left a job before. I never had another full-time job other than WWCO. Just then I heard my dad who was listening in on the extension downstairs say in a loud whisper, "Ask him how much they're going to pay you."

Oh yeah, I hadn't thought of that. "Uh, Gordon, uh…let me

ask you something here…uh, how much will I be paid for this job?"

He laughed again, "Oh, that's right we haven't talked about that. This will be good. How much do you make now?"

This will be good? I thought, what did he mean by that?

I knew exactly how much I made. I was pulling in a respectable $7,800 a year, that's $150 a week, plus I had a free gas trade that the station set up for me instead of giving me a raise that year. It was with a gas station 30 miles away. And at 30 cents a gallon, it wasn't worth the drive for the free gas. My dad, covering the mouthpiece once again, called up to me, "Tell him you make $170 a week."

Good old Dad, pumping up my wage, from $150 to $170 to help negotiate more money for me. It was a sly move I thought. Probably the way they do things in Washington all the time. "Uh, I make $170 a week, Gordon," I said with confidence.

"$170, huh." He laughed. There was a lot of laughing going on here, I thought.

"Let me just get my calculator." I heard him punching in some numbers. "Well, Dave or Tom, you'll be in AFTRA here and we have a minimum scale that we have to pay our disc jockeys."

This was way over my head…I heard "Dave" and "Tom" then blah blah blah something about "after" and then something about a "scale." A couple more stabs at his desktop calculator and he said, "We'll be paying you $26,500."

My dad made a strange noise on the extension phone, a combination of a gasp and a giddy laugh. I was confused. I had read about athletes getting a three-year deal, maybe this was going to be spread out over a few years.

"26,500…dollars…every year?" I said.

"Yes, $26-5 a year and you'll be paid for personal appearances and commercial endorsements which will bump that up over 30."

I said, "Oh, that will be fine. Thank Gordon you, Mr. Peil, me good, I'll phone talk in the tomorrow." There was a confused silence on his end of the line and then with a smile in his voice he said, "OK then."

There was a stunned quiet in the Cipriano house on Sunnyside Avenue for a couple of beats and then I think I screamed first and I think my dad screamed and then my mother screamed and then the three of us all screamed. What the hell? Who in the world makes twenty-six thousand dollars in one year? My Dad made $15,000 and that was a family wage. It felt like I had won the lottery and I was in some sort of shock. I caught my breath and called Mike Joseph in Providence and said, "Mike, thank you so much for the offer, but I'm sorry something came up and I'm going to Washington, D.C., instead."

He was not happy. "Washington, D.C.? Well, if that's what you want. But I'm telling you, you're making a big mistake."

I thanked him for his thoughts and wished him well. And all I could think of was, what would it be like to move to the nation's capital? I couldn't fathom it.

My last day in Connecticut was a Sunday. I went to my brother's house for one of our big, Italian, middle of the day family dinners. When it was time to leave, after so many hugs and kisses, I remember backing out of the driveway looking at my folks, my brother Henry, his wife Eileen and my little niece and nephew, Christine and Mark. All of our emotions were right on the surface. You could see it on everyone's face. A mixture of happiness, sadness, apprehension, and pride. My car, a Chevy

Camaro, was loaded with most of my stuff and enough of my mom's tomato sauce to get me through the next few months. I was leaving home for the first time. Six years had gone by since I called my favorite disc jockey at WWCO. When I stepped out of that ancient elevator on 65 Bank Street, I stepped into the land of imagination, the wonderful world of radio. I met the right people at the right place and the right time to help a 14-year-old kid make his dreams come true. It was magic. With one last look, I beeped my horn, waved goodbye to my family, and said goodnight to WWCO. Then I hit the road for my new job at NBC.

My Mom and Dad, 1939.

This is half of my family, Mom's side, that came to our house for dinner on Sunday afternoons.

With my big brother Hank

I was 15 years old, running the WWCO remote broadcast equipment for Joe Sherwood, behind me.

Exchange Place, downtown Waterbury. The building in the middle is 65 Bank St., WWCO.

Ron Gregory in the WWCO FM studio. I used to hide from the bosses beneath those turntables.

Tim Clark in the WWCO AM studio at 65 Bank St.

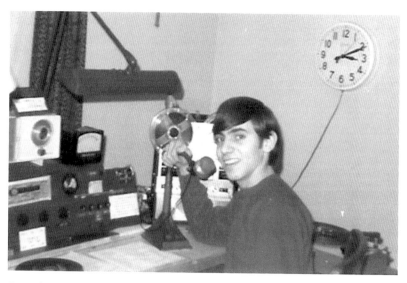

At my home radio station, WOLF in Oakville, 15 years old.

The one and only Johnny Walker from WWCO. Later at Q107 he called himself
Uncle Johnny.

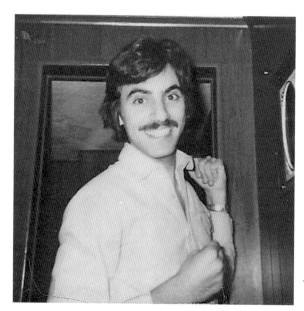

Me as Tom Collins just before leaving for NBC in Washington, D.C.

Me as Joe Cipriano one month later with my new "NBC" look.

Gordon Peil, my new boss at WKYS in Washington. He called me "Goomba."

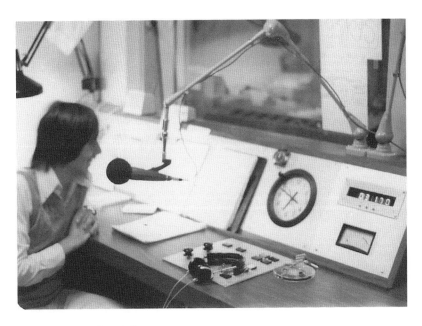

In the WKYS studio, 1975.

The first time I met Stoney Richards, I knew we would be pals forever.

Stoney and Ann outside of NBC at 4001 Nebraska Ave. NW, Washington, D.C.

WKYS Picnic. Left to right: Skip McCloskey, Lundy Baker, Jack Casey, Donnie Simpson, Candy Wessling, Melissa Huston, Ann Gudelsky, Joe Cipriano, Stoney Richards and Barbara Grieco

The WKYS Disco deejays. Donnie Simpson, me, Jeff Leonard and Stoney Richards

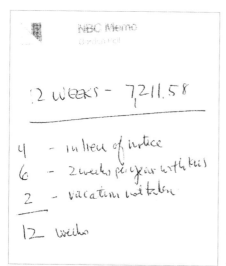

The first time I was ever fired, Gordon wrote my severance payout on his memo pad.

Stoney and I were both out of work, but Ann still hung with us.

The Jewish girl marries the
Italian Catholic boy, May
19, 1979.

I love this photo from our wedding. Behind us on the left, Ann's Uncle Jerry is
singing his heart out, that's my mom behind the cake and Ann's dad on the right,
behind her.

> I finally got back to being a Top 40 deejay at Q107. We were number one in Washington, D.C.

With Q107's "Remarkable Mouth" girl, Chris DeLisle, at a Q107 appearance.

KHTZ Los Angeles staff, left to right, Charlie Tuna, Boyd R. Britton, Larry Kahn, unknown, me photo bombing in the back, our GM Bob Moore, Ken Noble, Stoney Richards photo bombing from the back row, our P.D. Jim Conlee and Dave Skyler.

Barbara, Stoney, and Ann celebrating New Years Eve together in our new city, Los Angeles, 1981.

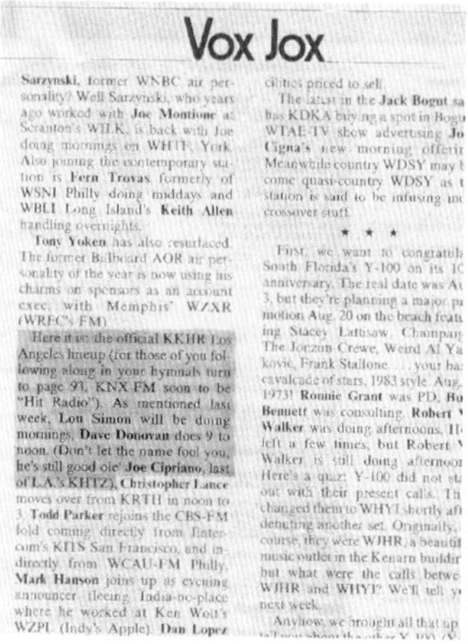

Vox Jox

Sarzynski, former WNBC air personality? Well Sarzynski, who years ago worked with **Joe Montione** at Scranton's WILK, is back with Joe doing mornings on WHTF, York. Also joining the contemporary station is **Fern Trovas**, formerly of WSNI Philly doing middays and WBLI Long Island's **Keith Allen** handling overnights.

Tony Yoken has also resurfaced. The former Billboard AOR air personality of the year is now using his charms on sponsors as an account exec. with Memphis' WZXR (WREC's FM).

Here it is: the official KKHR Los Angeles lineup (for those of you following along in your hymnals turn to page 93, KNX FM soon to be "Hit Radio"). As mentioned last week, **Lou Simon** will be doing mornings, **Dave Donovan** does 9 to noon. (Don't let the name fool you, he's still good ole' **Joe Cipriano**, last of L.A.'s KHTZ). **Christopher Lance** moves over from KRTH in noon to 3. **Todd Parker** rejoins the CBS-FM fold coming directly from Entercom's KIIS San Francisco, and indirectly from WCAU-FM Philly. **Mark Hanson** joins up as evening announcer fleeing India-no-place where he worked at Ken Wolt's WZPL (Indy's Apple). **Dan Lopez**

cilities priced to sell.

The latest in the **Jack Bogut** sa has KDKA buying a spot in Bogu WTAE-TV show advertising **Jo Cigna's** new morning offerir Meanwhile country WDSY may b come quasi-country WDSY as t station is said to be infusing inc crossover stuff.

* * *

First, we want to congratul South Florida's Y-100 on its 1C anniversary. The real date was Au 3, but they're planning a major pr motion Aug. 20 on the beach featu ing Stacey Lattisaw, Champaig The Jonzun Crewe, Weird Al Ya kovic, Frank Stallone . . . your ba cavalcade of stars, 1983 style. Aug, 1973! **Ronnie Grant** was PD, **Bu Bennett** was consulting, **Robert Walker** was doing afternoons. H left a few times, but Robert Walker is still doing afternoor Here's a quiz: Y-100 did not st out with their present calls. Th changed them to WHYI shortly aft denoting another set. Originally, course, they were WJHR, a beautif music outlet in the Kenarn buildir but what were the calls betwe WJHR and WHYI? We'll tell y next week.

Anyhow, we brought all that up

Announcing KKHR a little too early. KIIS FM stole our thunder. Billboard Magazine.

KKHR deejays, Chris Lance, Lou Simon, Mark Hanson, Todd Parker and me, Dave Donovan. Our P.D., Ed Scarborough, is in the middle.

Madonna and me at the KKHR "Desperately Seeking Susan" world premiere.

GOOMBA

Washington, D.C., transformed my life. I lived there for five years, and during that time I worked at two different radio stations, got fired for the first time, met my best friend, and also met my best girl. I learned about the kind of man I wanted to be and how I wanted to live my life. You could say I grew up in Washington. Most people have that kind of experience in college, but I did it another way. Sort of like on-the-job training. My education took place in a beautiful, vibrant, exciting city, the nation's capital. It was the mid-seventies, the Vietnam War was finally over, President Richard Nixon had resigned from office after the Watergate scandal, the country had started to gear up for its bicentennial celebration. This was, absolutely, the big time.

After that long drive from Connecticut, pulling into the city was like a dream. All the monuments were lit up in bright white lights against the dark sky. Honestly, it took my breath away. Or maybe that was the weather. Have you ever been to Washington in the summer? At nine o'clock in the evening the temperature was 99 degrees and the humidity was 99 percent. It was like being under water, I was gasping for air. Coming from the Northeast I didn't have air conditioning in my car but after that first night, I decided to get a new car, with air conditioning, as soon as possible. I took a quick tour of the city, then went back to my hotel room in Georgetown and cranked up the air to a cool 68 degrees.

The next day, I reported for work at 4001 Nebraska Avenue. The NBC News Bureau was based in the same building as the radio station, along with the local television studios of WRC-TV. Radio was in the basement along with WRC-AM and my new home, WKYS-FM. My first day on the job I saw the one and only David Brinkley in the hallway, the anchor of the NBC Nightly News. I had just walked by his picture in the lobby. He actually said "hello" to me. I couldn't wait to tell my parents. "Meet the Press" was broadcast just up the stairs from our radio studio. There was even a commissary down the hall with a chef making fresh food each day. Everything about the place was "first class," but I was still a "coach class" kind of guy. I had a lot to learn.

Right away I had to get used to a new name. When my boss, Gordon, told me they were going to change it up, I said that was fine, I had never used "Cipriano" on the air, anyway. But my last name wasn't the problem. He liked "Cipriano." He didn't like "David." Like so many things at the network level, my new name was a group decision between Gordon and the consultant, Bob Henabery. Apparently it took hours and hours of debate before they came up with the answer. They liked the "oh" sound at the end of Cipriano and thought "Joe" fit perfectly. It was catchy. That's how I became Joe Cipriano. Joseph is my middle name, but they weren't even aware of that at the time. For the next few weeks, walking around the building, whenever anyone called out to me, "Joe!" I wouldn't respond. "Joe? Hey Joe!" "Oh, yeah… what?" I just couldn't wrap my head around the idea that they were talking to ME.

Then there was the studio. At NBC the disc jockeys didn't play their own records. They had engineers who sat in another room, running the commercials, jingles, and turntables. We called them "board-ops." It highlighted just how different small-town Waterbury radio was compared to big city, Washington, D.C., radio.

The on-air personality and board-op faced one another, sitting at our own consoles, separated by a thick glass window, and every time we wanted to talk to each other, we had to push the intercom button. Whenever I wanted the engineer to start up a record during my on-air rap, I had to give him a signal by pointing at him, cueing him for the next element. I was used to running my own show, with all the controls at my fingertips making last minute adjustments, but now, working at a union station, all I was allowed to do was turn my microphone on and off and adjust the volume of my headphones. Timing was more critical than ever.

Fortunately, the guy I was hired to replace was still around at the station, happy to show me how it all worked. He was moving on to another position at NBC, giving up radio to work full-time upstairs in television. He was a big bear of a guy, with a huge smile that showed off the space between his two front teeth. When we first met, I went to shake hands, but he pushed my arm to the side, grabbed me tight, practically lifted me off the ground, and then planted a wet kiss on my forehead. I thought, is that what you do in the big city? But no, that's what you do if you're Willard Scott, the most warm, wonderful, bundle of love person you could ever hope to meet.

I spent one week with Willard, the up-and-coming weatherman and future "Today Show" contributor. I had been hired to take over his midday shift, ten a.m. to two p.m. Later, after his show, I followed him to the commissary where he stopped to hug every single woman who came our way, giving them a big kiss on their forehead. Men, too! Willard was an equal opportunity kisser. There was no fear of sexual harassment or political correctness. People loved bumping into Willard. Down-to-earth, kind, friendly, that's the sort of guy I wanted to emulate. Someone people were happy to see. I never, ever, forgot that. Even today, when I walk into a room, I try to always have a smile on my face.

I embraced everything about my new city, going to museums, eating at all the ethnic restaurants, I didn't even mind getting lost around those crazy traffic circles. Not much, anyway. Even though D.C. is big, I was impressed by how green it all was, with plenty of open space, parks, and sprawling lawns. Because there's a height limit to the buildings downtown, it didn't feel overwhelming to me, unlike New York or Chicago. On my own for the first time, Washington was a good fit, almost like a small town. It felt comfortable. When it came time to find a place to live, I went out to the suburbs, something else that felt more manageable to me. Our afternoon guy at the radio station, Eddie Edwards, took me under his wing, and suggested I move out to his apartment complex in Wheaton, Maryland. With no idea where else to go, that's exactly what I did, renting a brand-new, modern, one-bedroom. I didn't have any furniture so I popped into a local chain store and bought the entire living room set they had on display in the showroom, complete with a very '70s orange shag rug and a brown plaid sofa made out of what the salesperson told me was the fabric of the future, Herculon.

Now it was time to get down to work. I had been on the air since I was 16 years old so that part was great, I was confident I could do the job. I was so happy to be in a top ten market that every day felt fresh and exciting. But I wasn't playing the Top 40 hits anymore. I knew when I was hired, the station was going to change formats. It happened one week after I got there. WKYS-FM turned into "Disco Stereo, 93-K-Y-S." Yep, disco. We played it all. "YMCA" by the Village People, Gloria Gaynor and "I Will Survive," Donna Summer, ABBA, Barry White, The Commodores, so many others. The station even paid for me to take dance lessons so I could do "The Hustle" like Van McCoy. We mixed those songs in with jazz tunes from Grover Washington Junior, George Benson, and Manhattan Transfer. That kind of format had never been done before. It was eclectic, unique, and

completely surprised me when we quickly leaped to the top of
the ratings, beating out every other established station in the city.
Two years later, when our ratings started to sag, along came John
Travolta in the movie "Saturday Night Fever," dressed up in that
white suit, dancing to the Bee Gees. The film was such a huge hit
it helped put us back on top again. But for now, that summer of
1975, we were the first 24-hour disco station in the country and
we killed the competition.

On top of all that, the promotions department at the station
set me up with a weekly gig at a hotel, just across the Potomac
River, in Crystal City, Virginia. I hosted a live show every Sunday
night from nine until midnight, and earned more money in those
three hours than I did for an entire week back at WWCO. Those
paychecks actually stacked up on the desk in my apartment. Life
was good and about to get even better.

A few months after I started at NBC the station hired a new
morning man, Stoney Richards from KIIS-AM in Los Angeles. I
couldn't understand why anyone in his right mind would leave a
radio gig in L.A., so I was anxious to meet this guy. From day one,
we were pretty much inseparable. Stoney is a writer, an actor, and
has a great sense of humor. At least I think he's funny, probably
because we laugh at all the same things. I had never worked with
anyone who prepared for his show as thoroughly as Stoney did,
certainly not me. He was on the air from six to ten in the morning
and then I took over with my shift. Except for those days when
I ran late. Unlike Stoney, I never got to work early. I always cut it
down to the very last second. I did the same thing at WWCO in
Connecticut. Like that time I thought I could make it to Arby's and
back while I was on the air. What an idiot! But I had a good reason
for doing it that way. I thought if I got to the station too early, even
five minutes early, it would ruin my show, my spontaneity, change
the momentum and excitement I had going for me.

I know exactly where that idea got burned into my twisted brain. It came from a TV Show in the '60s called, "Good Morning World," a sitcom about two Los Angeles morning DJs. I loved the opening sequence of that show. Every week one of the disc jockeys woke up to the clock alarm, jumped out of bed, then ran to his car. He drove down Mulholland Drive to the radio station, raced up the stairs, and dashed into the studio. Just as the clock ticked the last second to the top of the hour, he reached for the microphone and flicked the switch to say, "Good Morning World," and the theme music would start. I wanted that. That was big-time radio to me, exciting, and dangerous. It worked in Connecticut, but I only had a ten-minute drive back then and living in a small town, there wasn't any rush-hour traffic.

In Washington, I thought I had it planned out perfectly. It took me 30 minutes to drive from my apartment in Wheaton, Maryland, to the station at NBC. I cut it down to the last second but I couldn't predict the traffic. So, OK, I was late to work more times than I like to admit, but being the time freak I am, I knew EXACTLY how late I was. I had an excuse for every time, but not surprisingly that didn't go over well with my boss. Truth is, I was an immature 20-year-old kid who liked to gamble with the clock. Finally, Gordon called me into his office.

"Goomba, I want to talk to you."

Yes, he called me Goomba, and I didn't mind the reference. He also once told a reporter that he discovered me after I had fallen off of my father's fruit cart, another reference to my Italian heritage. Remember, those were the days before people talked about being politically correct. Anyway, I went to his office, with another excuse ready to go.

"Goomba, I don't know what to do with you. You can't seem to get into work on time. What is the matter with you?"

"Gordon, I just got hung up behind a stupid truck today, or I would have been here on time."

"Well, this can't go on. I don't know what else to do, so I've decided…to call your mother."

"What!? Call my mother??"

"Yes, maybe she can talk some sense into you."

I knew Gordon wasn't going to call my mother, but he had made his point. I was acting like a child. Many 20-year-olds exhibit that kind of behavior and the worst that happens most of the time is they're late for a college class, but when you're a 20-year-old, late for your radio show on NBC's multimillion-dollar broadcasting property in the nation's capital, a few people notice. It was time to grow up, to act like a professional, but I had a hard time taking that last step. I think meeting Stoney had a lot to do with changing my mind. We were such good friends and honestly, I didn't want him to be mad at me. Besides, I finally admitted to myself that it was rude for me to be late for my show. That meant Stoney had to stay on the air longer until I ran in the door. And then there was one more incentive for me to shape up. I guess it was also possible, I may have been just a little bit worried that Gordon might actually call my mom, after all. So out of respect for Stoney, and nightmares about Mom chasing me down Wisconsin Avenue with a wooden spoon, I made my choice. I was never late again.

At the ripe old age of 21, I decided to take myself more seriously, become more dependable, even dress a little sharper. I was ready to become the kind of man I hoped to be, a good change to make since I was about to meet the most important person in my life, my future wife.

It started out like any other day. I was on my way to the

commissary, during one of those long disco songs, when I bumped into a pretty girl in the hallway. I introduced myself, thinking she would be incredibly impressed to meet the famous deejay "Joe Cipriano," but apparently she had been living under a rock somewhere and had never heard of me. Poor girl, I thought, probably doesn't get out much. She told me her name was Ann Gudelsky, a local girl from Bethesda, Maryland, and it was her first day on the job. She was a writer for All News WRC-AM radio, so I gallantly escorted her to the newsroom. The FM studio was right next door to the AM station, and we got to see a lot of each other. I did my best to get Ann to notice me, dropping in after hours when she was on the overnight shift, even coming in early when she moved to morning drive time. After more than a few tries, Ann finally agreed to have dinner with me and we started dating. A college-educated, nice Jewish girl from the big city going out with a high-school educated, Catholic boy from a small town. Add some luck, mixed in with a little charm, and the timing would turn out to be just right. Even though our backgrounds were so different, we shared the same values. Both of our parents were together forever, my mom and dad were married for 60 years. Ann's parents made it to 56 years before her dad passed away. We were in good company. Stoney was also dating a girl who worked at NBC, Barbara Grieco. Together, the four of us became the best of friends, sharing a connection that continues to this day.

Up until now, my life had been one fantastic ride. A great family, good friends, my dream job, even meeting the girl of my dreams, but it was about to take a turn. It was 1978 and out of the blue, Stoney was let go from the station. Rumors started circulating that NBC was going to change formats, disco was dead, smooth jazz was in. I had always been a high-energy kind of disc jockey playing the hits whether it was country, Top 40, or disco. Now Gordon wanted the deejays to slow down, relax,

be mellow. Probably the last word anyone would use to describe me is "mellow." They changed the name of the station from Disco Stereo to "Ninety Three Nine, Uptown." I gave it a shot in the new format but it wasn't natural, so I was shocked when my engineer, Stu Bullman, told me he heard the entire staff was getting fired, except for me. One day during my show, Gordon called on the hot line and said he wanted to see me at the end of the day. Well, I thought, this is it, Stu was right, Gordon is going to let me in on the big rumor. But when I walked into his office, that's not how it went.

"Goomba," he said sadly. The way he said it, I knew right away.

He gently carried on to tell me I just had too much energy, too much personality, for the new format. Stu had it wrong. Everyone was staying, but me. Now, I was out of work like Stoney. I had seen other jocks get fired, but I never thought it would happen to me. I got a severance check worth 12 weeks' pay and a handshake.

Now what? I wasn't prepared for this to happen. I couldn't run home to Mom and Dad. What a strange and absolutely frightening feeling. But most of all, I was sad. It hurt. I was singled out, thrown out, while everyone else I knew stayed. They didn't want me to come here every day anymore. I wouldn't be allowed to park in that lot anymore. I didn't work for NBC anymore. It was my first ride down on the roller coaster of life and, honestly, it was awful.

In the first place, I hate roller coasters. That terrible feeling you get in the pit of your stomach when the car drops from the top of the track, and plunges to the ground, that's how I felt, all of the time. My stomach was in knots. I had my family, my friends, and Annie to lean on, but I knew it was up to me to get out of that jam. At least I was single, no wife, no kids, no mortgage. It was

just me, my life, my problem, my responsibility. So much of what happens around us is out of our control. In radio, like any other job, when a new boss comes in, there are going to be changes. The problem is, even if you are doing your best, you might get blown out anyway. In my case, the format changed and I didn't fit in anymore. It happens all the time in radio but when it happened to me I felt lost. It was hard to know what to do with myself when I didn't have anywhere to go in the morning. How do you fill the hours? How do you find a new job? How do you keep from getting depressed? I am an upbeat, positive person. I like being around people. I need to be around people. But I didn't feel like that after I got fired. Mostly, I wanted to be alone. It wasn't that I felt sorry for myself, not much anyway. I just needed to think. What would my dad do? What about my brother, Henry? They were two of the most responsible people I knew but they didn't know anything about the radio business. I needed a job, fast. I knew that if I was going to make something positive happen, I had to work on it, relentlessly. Even now, I do the same thing, for almost any new goal I hope to achieve. If I want to go after a new gig, learn a sport, write a book, whatever it is, I give it my complete attention for one hour a day, minimum. Of course, after I was fired, I had all day to work on finding a new job. So that's what I did. I mailed out airchecks and hit the phones, nonstop. I had to make something happen.

Several months earlier, Ann had gotten a new job at WJLA-TV, Channel Seven, as an assignment editor and news writer. She was as surprised as I was that NBC had let me go but she was always on my side, absolutely positive that something good would turn up. I didn't have long to worry. A few weeks after I was fired, I was offered a job at WIND radio in Chicago, one of those cities I dreamed about as a kid. Fantastic! We made the decision to move there together. Ann was excited too, looking forward to working in television in Chicago, when I suddenly changed my

mind. Something just didn't feel right so I took a risk and turned down that job. My intuition paid off. Six months later WIND dropped its format for All Talk and I would have been out of work. Again. Instead, I ended up staying in Washington, looking for any radio gig in town.

Even with all of this uncertainty in my career, I knew what I wanted to do in my personal life. I had been going out with Ann for two and a half years when I made the best decision of my life. It was Christmas Eve, 1978. We were at my parents' house in Connecticut, about to go to my cousin's for a big family party. It was just the two of us at home, my parents had already left, when I suggested we each open one gift. I have no idea what she gave me, I was much too excited to remember. I gave her a small box that she thought might be a bracelet, and when she opened it, there was a diamond ring. I got down on one knee and asked her to marry me. Luckily, she said yes! It was a perfect night. There was a light snow falling when we left the house to go to my cousin Betty Ann's. The entire family was there, aunts and uncles, cousins, my brother Henry and his family. Everybody was in on the secret proposal and was waiting for our arrival. A cheer went up as we walked into the house and we drank champagne with our huge Italian feast that night. It was a perfect evening and I could not have been happier. She is my one and only true love.

After a wonderful Christmas in Connecticut we were back in D.C. and I was still out of work. In desperation I called WRQX, the album rock station owned by ABC, to see if there were any openings. It wasn't my style at all, but I couldn't afford to wait for the perfect job. It was the kind of station where they played long album cuts, one after the other, where the jocks hardly said anything, but the afternoon guy had just left for a job in New York. There was an opening, and luckily, they gave me the show on a trial basis. What a relief. I was back on the radio.

Up until now, I was the kind of deejay who talked up records and said funny stuff on the air. Now I was in a radio format where all I said was, "That was Led Zeppelin, and before that was Foghat, and before that was…" aw crap, give me a break. At least I had a job and even better, Stoney was on the air with me again. After I got the afternoon shift at WRQX, I passed along Stoney's tape to the program director and he hired him for the night shift. Believe me, I was happy to have a paycheck but I wasn't content to play it safe. I was the same ambitious person I had always been. So I spent most of my time trying to figure out how to get back into Top 40 radio. And then it fell into my lap.

HARDBALL

Working in radio can be a very risky business because there is no job security. Sure, there may be some radio personalities who feel safe about their jobs, people like Ryan Seacrest or Howard Stern. But even the famous Don Imus ran into trouble when he made a racially offensive comment on the air in 2007 about the Rutgers women's basketball team. Without any safety net, I think most deejays, like me, are just happy to be on the air, with a gig in broadcasting. If it's not the perfect station, or format, you learn to make the best of it.

So there I was, at WRQX, playing those album cuts that went on forever. No more Top 40 radio for me. Plenty of time to pop out for lunch while a record was spinning on the turntable. No, not really. I had learned my lesson on that one. But I wasn't about to give up on trying to get back to what I enjoyed the most, playing the hits. I wanted out. I was frustrated, bored, and uninspired. I didn't care what went on at the station because I just wasn't interested.

I was so out of touch with everything, that it came as a complete surprise when I walked into work one day and heard our boss had been fired. I had no idea he was about to be let go. All of a sudden I started listening to what everyone had to say,

very closely. I heard ABC was changing formats but no one knew what was coming. Country? Classical? What now? Then word came down the station was going to go Top 40. Are you kidding me? Instead of hoping to break out of there, I was desperate to stay. Rumor had it the new boss was the one and only Al Brady Law, a brilliant program director who had worked in New York, Miami, and Boston. Suddenly I was in the perfect situation to impress the famous programmer, except for one tiny problem. For the past four years I had been playing disco and now album rock. How was I going to show Al I could do the Top 40 gig?

I took a risk. On my own I dropped the album rock format, "before that…and before that…and before that…" and started talking to the listeners again, really talking, having fun, making jokes. What did I have to lose? I figured he was going to come in and fire everyone anyway, so why not have a good time while I tried to save my job and show off some of my skills.

Al came to us from WHDH in Boston and he brought along his news director, Doug Limerick. Doug is a great guy, originally from the South, with a beautiful voice. He is the consummate professional with a slightly twisted sense of humor. Just my kind of guy. We hit it off right away. In our conversations, it came out that I was from Connecticut, had worked in Top 40 most of my life, including WDRC in Hartford. Doug was familiar with the Big-D, because it was one of the great music stations in New England. I was hoping he would put in a good word for me with Al.

I met my new boss for the first time at a staff meeting, sitting around a huge table in the conference room. Everyone was there, the deejays, engineers, and office personnel. We sat waiting for

about 20 minutes when Al finally burst through the door. He was taller than me, about five ten, with a big belly, a thick mustache that covered his mouth, and he had a head full of black curly hair, shaped like an Afro. He immediately took over the room. All attention was on Al as he slowly scanned the table and said, "We are taking this station Top 40 and we are gonna kick ass! I'd like to say that one year from now, we'll all be sitting here together at this table, but I gotta tell ya, I doubt it."

Later that week Al fired every single jock at the station except for Stoney and me.

All I could think was, God bless Doug Limerick. I'm pretty sure he saved my life at ABC. Thanks, Doug. But hot damn! I was a Top 40 jock again. The new Q-107 went on the air on April 16, 1979, just about one month away from my wedding date. Our first day on the air, Ann was home sick with the flu and she taped my entire shift. It was such a big deal to me, I still have that recording all these years later. We had a huge budget from ABC, all the money we could ever dream of, to help launch the new Q. We gave away cars, trips, concert tickets, and cash. Every Thursday, every week, was Thousand Dollar Thursday. You never knew when it was going to happen, but sometime during the day one of us deejays played the song "Hey Jude," and caller number one-oh-seven would win the money. I was having fun again.

There was even an attention-getting television commercial created for all the ABC radio stations by the advertising geniuses Chuck Blore and Don Richmond. It was called "The Remarkable Mouth." It started with a shot of this beautiful woman, with long shaggy hair, wearing a tight T-shirt, of course, with Q-107 in big letters across her chest. Chris DeLisle was her name, she had clear

blue eyes, and a perfect smile covered in bright red lipstick. The camera started out wide, and she said, "Here's something I know you'll like," then the shot slowly zoomed in extremely tight, so you could only see her mouth. Next, you heard each disc jockey say something, our voices coming out of her mouth while her lips moved in perfect sync to everything we said. Believe me, in 1979, that commercial was the coolest thing anyone had ever seen on TV. She was HOT! And so was the New Q.

My buddy Doug did the morning show with Dude Walker. They were absolutely brilliant together. Dave Thomson handled middays. I got the afternoon drive time slot from two to six, a step up from middays for me, oh and remember my old buddy Johnny Walker, from WWCO? I carried his aircheck from Q105 in Tampa into Al's office one day and said, "Stick this in the tape deck and crank it up." Johnny was using the name "Uncle Johnny" in Tampa and his act was outrageous. Johnny liked to say, "Everybody has someone crazy in their family and that's me. The whacked-out uncle." Al loved him and Johnny grabbed the early evening shift, from six to ten. Sandy Weaver, our first female jock, had the late-night shift. By now, Stoney had made a big decision to leave radio to concentrate on acting full-time. I missed working with him but I understood why he made that choice. Even though Stoney had left the station, he was still in town to be one of the groomsmen at my wedding. My brother Henry was my best man.

Ann and I got married May 19, 1979, at the L'Enfant Plaza Hotel in Washington, D.C., Ann's hometown. Her parents planned it all, there was a band, great food, beautiful flowers, it was one big party! All of our friends were there from NBC, ABC, Channel 7,

and both families, of course. To this day, more than 30 years later, people still tell us how much fun they had at our wedding. It's a great memory.

In our very first ratings book, Q-107 buried all the other stations in the city. I had struggled through the past few months, when I was fired from NBC, and then when I took a job that wasn't the right fit. But I never lost faith in myself. I was back in Top 40 radio, the number one afternoon deejay at the number one station in town.

Doing the afternoon show from two p.m. to six p.m., I had plenty of time in the morning to pursue a brand-new adventure, voice-over work. Out of the blue, I started to be asked to voice local and regional commercials in Washington. I didn't know much about the voice-over world, but I quickly found out it's a nice place to visit. I worked for clients like Garfinckel's Department Store, and Woodward & Lothrop, classy ads designed by the Denenberg Agency in D.C. The owner and creative director, Elliot Denenberg, liked my voice and started using me on a few accounts for car dealerships and other retail radio and TV work. Plus before my shift at the Q, I made personal appearances for the station at high schools and charity functions, just like the kind of events I used to go to at WWCO in Connecticut. After my shift at six p.m., I either went to another meeting for the station or went out to dinner with Ann, Stoney, and Barbara. It was a great balance of work and personal satisfaction. Getting fired from NBC was quickly turning into a distant memory. Those terrible feelings were long gone.

Moving into the 1980s, the Q continued to grow. As we hit the one-year anniversary of the station and my marriage, I became

more and more interested in a voice-over career. I thought being in radio teed it up perfectly. I could pursue VO while my radio show paid the bills. I became aware of the big network voices like Ernie Anderson, Danny Dark, and others who lived in Los Angeles. Dreaming about that kind of career gave me a new goal to reach for in my career. I talked it over with Ann, and just like that we both decided where we were headed next.

For as long as I can remember I wanted to work in Los Angeles. If I was ever going to get a chance at national voice-over work, or doing promos for networks, I thought it could only happen in L.A. We were a team and Ann was all in, ready to find new opportunities in her own career as a TV news writer and producer. But I wouldn't allow myself to move across the country without a job in radio already lined up. I had no interest in being another out of work, starving actor/voice-over guy in L.A. The plan was simple: I would mail out airchecks to radio stations in L.A., hoping that someone would take the bait. I loved Q-107. It was high-energy fun with great music. I knew how fortunate I was to get that job. But I'm not the kind of person who sits still for long. Like my dad, I'm always thinking of how I can make a particular situation even better and looking for what's next for me down the road. I made it my priority to get to Los Angeles and as always I tried to work one hour each day on making it happen. After six months of sending out tapes, I had an offer.

I got a call from Jim Conlee at KHTZ radio in Los FREAKING Angeles.

"Joe? We listened to your tape and really like what you're doing. We want to hire you at K-HITS."

My head nearly burst. This was different from the call I got from Gordon when I was still living at home in Connecticut. Back then I was a kid who would have gone anywhere without a thought about how I would get there, how much I would make, or even how I would live. This time I wasn't alone, I had Annie by my side. I knew exactly what part of L.A. I wanted to live in, and I knew I would have to take a pay cut to get there but I thought I could make up the difference in voice-overs. I thought I was prepared for everything. But wouldn't you know, that roller coaster was heading my way again, ready to take me down. Two seats please!

I had a new boss at Q-107. Al Brady Law had moved on to WABC in New York, and the new Program Director was Alan Burns, young, hip, and cool. We got along well, and I was positive he would be happy for me. The next day, I could barely wait till my shift was over to tell him about my offer.

"Alan, I have a wonderful opportunity. I've been offered the dream job I've been waiting for in Los Angeles. KHTZ wants to hire me for afternoons. I love Q but I've been working towards this my whole life. I want to be fair and give you two or three weeks' notice. Whatever you need."

Alan was surprisingly expressionless. He just looked at me and said, "You signed a letter of intent to enter into a contract with us. We won't let you go."

My mouth dropped along with my stomach. Of course I remembered signing that letter, but at the time I was told it was only to stop me and the other jocks from taking a job with the local competition, at one of the other stations in Washington. All radio

stations do that kind of thing. I thought that was fair. The execs at ABC didn't want to be in competition with talent they cultivated.

He said, "ABC owns two stations in Los Angeles, and we don't want you in competition with them, either."

"You've got to be kidding me, right?" I was stunned.

"No Joe. I'm serious. We're playing hardball here."

That hurt me. I loved that station and everyone there, including Alan. But as far as I knew, this was my once in a lifetime opportunity. They wanted to lock me into five years at Q-107. I was 25 years old.

"Alan, you want me to wait until I'm 30 years old to have the chance to follow this dream?"

His answer, "Hardball, Joe."

I didn't blame Alan, I knew he was doing his job, but I needed help to figure this out. Were they right? Did they own me for the next five years? I had no idea. I had to hire a lawyer to find out the answer.

My attorney's name was Julian Tepper. I didn't know anything about him except that he was a friend of a friend. He normally did litigation work for the government and he was looking forward to doing something different. He seemed like a sharp guy to me. From the beginning he told me, "I can take care of this for you. Don't worry."

I called Jim in L.A. to tell him what was going on and was surprised to find out he already knew. A huge corporation like ABC has plenty of lawyers on staff. Sadly, some of them were

working against me. KHTZ radio had received a "cease and desist" order to stop negotiating with me. Any more discussions, and ABC would take legal action against KHTZ. Damn, this really was hardball.

But Jim was calm. He told me not to worry. "Listen, Joe, this is big corporation shit. You work it out and I'll keep a shift open for you. Good luck!"

Julian put in a couple of weeks of back and forth arguments, but he wasn't getting anywhere. Finally he said, "Joe, they'll keep stonewalling until you run out of money. You're never going to be able to match the amount that ABC can put into this fight with all the lawyers it has. There's only one thing left you can do. We have to use what they want so badly, against them."

I didn't know where he was headed so he explained. "They want you on the air. Let's take that away from them. Go into Alan's office and tell him you can't handle it anymore. The stress of all this is just too much and you need time off, without pay. You can't do your show, you need a leave of absence."

Oh man, I never would have thought of doing something like that. It wasn't my nature. It was sneaky. And it was freakin' brilliant. Julian's advice went against everything my parents had taught me about being responsible and doing a good job. Making the decision even more difficult, we were in the middle of a ratings sweep, the most important time of all, for radio and television stations. If your company comes out number one in the ratings, it means millions of dollars in advertising revenue for the station. But I had to trust Julian. Besides, his advice wasn't far from the truth. I was miserable, stressed out, and felt nearly hopeless.

I figured this was the only way off that roller coaster. So right before my shift, the next day, I did it. I walked into Alan's office and told him I needed a break. He nearly fell off his chair.

"You can't leave. We're in the middle of ratings."

"I know Alan, I feel awful. But my health is more important."

"Listen, do your shift today and I'll talk to you after you get off the air."

I was as nervous as I have ever been in my life, but I was also determined. This was war. Chew on that, fucking hardball.

After my shift I went into Alan's office. His boss, Ernie Fears, was there, too.

"Joe, we're going to let you go to Los Angeles, but first you have to agree to stay with us through the end of the November ratings. Then you can leave."

I don't know how I managed to stay so composed but somehow I calmly answered, "That'll be just fine, Alan. No problem." I thanked Alan and Ernie, then called Julian for the biggest thanks of all.

L.A. HERE I COME! I was stoked! My last day on the air was a blast. I said goodbye to the Q-107 listeners, see ya on the Left Coast! The last song I played on the air in D.C. was "My Life," by Billy Joel.

Doug Limerick threw us a going-away party that night. Before we left town, Ann's parents had all their relatives over for another send-off later in the week. Early on in our relationship, my in-laws, Audrey and Albert Gudelsky, accepted me as part of

their family. Before we met, I'm sure they thought Ann would marry someone who was Jewish, maybe even a nice doctor or a lawyer. But she fell in love with me, a disc jockey, a Catholic boy, who never went to college. Her parents trusted me and I respected them. Ann's mom was full of energy and her dad was a wonderful, gentle soul. After the party, when we said goodnight, it suddenly hit me, I was taking their baby girl away from them. Moving her to the other side of the country. My father-in-law was a quiet, soft-spoken man but I could see he was choked up. As Ann and I walked to her childhood bedroom where we were spending our last night in Maryland, her dad called out to her, "I love you, baby."

I can't tell you how deeply I felt those words. As a parent now, I understand his sadness even more.

The next morning was a bright, new day. We flew up to Connecticut to say goodbye to my family, a little bit easier since I had been living away from home for the past six years. It was the end of November and we wouldn't be able to come back east for at least a few months, so we celebrated Christmas and Thanksgiving all in one. My mom outdid herself and woke up at four in the morning to put the turkey in the oven. We had all my favorite foods including cavatelli and pumpkin pie. She made Ann's favorite, too, apple pie. I have never, ever left home without Mom giving me a package of something she made from scratch. Since we were flying out to Los Angeles she didn't want to give me her sauce. She was afraid the container might leak on the plane. Instead we took a tin of her homemade Christmas cookies with a promise that Mom would send more later. We said our goodbyes the Saturday after Thanksgiving, then my big brother Hank drove us to New York for our flight to the West Coast.

I had booked two first-class tickets out of JFK Airport on American Airlines, nonstop to Los Angeles International. It was finally happening. We were on our way to L.A.

LOOKING FOR LUCK

I love to fly. Taking off, floating in the air, going to new places. I think that's why I like that movie "Catch Me If You Can." I probably just miss the days when it was more glamorous to fly. I still like to get dressed up when I travel, sports jacket, nice slacks, dress shoes. Sometimes I might wear a tie even though I may end up sitting next to someone wearing shorts and flip-flops. In this era of being treated like cattle when you travel, I think dressing up for a flight shows respect. Respect for the flight attendants, the pilots, and the airport crew. You may not believe this, but the respect is always returned. It's almost as if I've found a great little secret no one knows about. I get a smile instead of a sneer, a welcome instead of a grunt. I'm actually treated better and it makes the flight more enjoyable.

Flying to Los Angeles, in December of 1980, was still a classy way to travel. I had booked two first-class tickets, on an American Airlines 747. That was back when the upstairs of a 747 was a lounge and bar area. Very swanky. As far as I was concerned it was the only way to make our way to my dream destination, Los Angeles.

It was a bright, warm day when we landed in L.A. We caught a cab to the Hyatt Hotel on Wilshire Boulevard in downtown

L.A., a few blocks from the radio station. I was now working for the Greater Media Company, a much smaller outfit than the two networks I worked for in Washington, but it had some big-market stations. Surprisingly, KHTZ paid for our move to L.A. That was a big deal for us. It cost $8,000 to pack up and transport our stuff out west and remember, I took the new job at a pay cut. Someone once told me in L.A., "they pay you in sunshine," and that was okay with me.

I still hadn't met my new program director, Jim Conlee, in person. I had a lot of respect for him. He had kept a shift open for me during the entire legal mess, trying to get out of my ABC deal. But up until now we had only talked on the phone. We decided to meet at our hotel the day after Ann and I arrived. After working for NBC and ABC, I was used to powerful executives, wearing expensive suits. When Jim walked in, he looked a little rumpled, like he might have had a long night. His suit was a bit too big, his hair stuck out a little, I was surprised. But he was a great guy and I figured, this might just be the casual, West Coast lifestyle.

My first night on the air was not what I expected, either. It started out fine. The studios were beautiful. Each one had a Neumann microphone, absolutely top of the line. Everybody wanted to talk through a Neumann but not every station could afford to buy one. They sounded incredible. I was hired for the five to nine shift at night but first Jim wanted me to get used to the format by doing an overnight shift. That's when the unexpected happened.

I met the overnight jock, Daniel, who showed me the audio board. We talked for a bit, then before I took over I excused myself to use the bathroom. I ran straight to the toilet and immediately

tossed my cookies. That was the first and only time I have ever thrown up before going on the air. This was my big dream, yet here I was at 1:45 in the morning about to say, "Hello Los Angeles," and I was driving the porcelain bus on the floor in the bathroom.

By two a.m. I recovered, put on my headphones, cranked up the music, and flicked on the Neumann, lighting up the red blinking "ON AIR" sign. Then I said my first words on the radio since leaving D.C., "K-Hits 97…hello L.A.! My name's Joe Cipriano. I think we're gonna have a great time together!"

And we did. More than 30 years later, Los Angeles is still my home. The first place we lived was Pacific Palisades, close to the beach. It's a small town, nestled on the outside of the sprawling city that is L.A. It looked perfect, as if a movie director had designed the set and hired actors to live there. Most importantly, it fit the small-town feel that I craved. There was no indication that you were in a big city. On any given day young mothers pushed their baby strollers down the sidewalk, kids played at the park or walked to the local library, people smiled and waved to one another across the street. Local residents owned most of the stores: Mort's Deli, Harrington's Camera Shop, Benton's Sporting Goods. One afternoon I had just missed getting to the bank before it closed. I was about ten minutes late. The manager saw me try the door, came over, opened it up and let me in to take care of business. That had never happened to me in Washington. Every year the Chamber of Commerce elected an honorary mayor, always a celebrity. When we moved there, in the 1980s, there were Chevy Chase, Larry Hagman, and Dom DeLuise. More recently boxer Sugar Ray Leonard served as mayor. On the Fourth of July there's a parade down Sunset Boulevard with skydivers, marching bands,

and a huge fireworks display at night. We had cool ocean breezes during the day and on a quiet evening, we could hear waves crashing on the beach. Pacific Palisades was where we lived when our children, Dayna and Alex, were born. It was better than I ever imagined. My roller coaster ride seemed to have smoothed out.

Monday, December 8, 1980, was my first full night on the job at K-Hits. By seven that night, the office staff was gone and I was alone in the building. A few minutes after eight the Associated Press news wire started going nuts in the next room, ringing non-stop, spewing out pages and pages of some sort of bulletin. I grabbed the copy and this is what I saw:

> **BULLETIN (AP) (NEW YORK) — THERE'S A REPORT THAT JOHN LENNON HAS BEEN SHOT. IT HAPPENED IN NEW YORK, ON THE UPPER WEST SIDE. POLICE SAY A MAN TENTATIVELY IDENTIFIED AS THE FORMER BEATLE WAS SHOT AND WOUNDED AND HAS BEEN TAKEN IN A POLICE CAR TO ROOSEVELT HOSPITAL. A SUSPECT HAS BEEN TAKEN INTO CUSTODY. NO WORD JUST YET ON HOW SERIOUS IT IS.**

> *AP-MP-12-08-80*

I wasn't sure how they handled that sort of story in L.A. but back in D.C. we would break into the song that was currently playing to read an urgent news headline. There wasn't anyone around to ask, so I just did what I thought was right. I slowly brought down the volume on the song, then read the bulletin live on the air. When I finished, I grabbed a John Lennon song out of the rack and let it play. The phones went crazy. Some people

called to ask if it was true, others called with updates for me that they had heard on television. About ten minutes later there was another AP bulletin. Four words came across the wire:

JOHN LENNON SHOT DEAD

I tossed out the format and began to play all Lennon and Beatles songs the rest of the night. People called in by the hundreds. I thought it would be a good idea to let them express their grief, share their sorrow on the air. In my own little way, it seemed like I was doing something, at a time when there was really nothing any of us could do. It was a sad and emotional evening.

My time at KHTZ turned out to be as unpredictable as that first night. It was a mixture of joy and frustration. Charlie Tuna was our morning man, which was a real kick. He's a legendary disc jockey and I was thrilled to be on a station with him, in Los Angeles. But the format was unlike anything I had ever done before. We played soft rock hits, Dan Fogelberg, Billy Joel, James Taylor. The music was nice but the format of the station was extremely tight, almost every word we said on the air was overly controlled. Even the way we said the call letters was strictly formatted. There was a card in the studio with a visual example of the proper way to say the name of the station:

K

H

T   HITS 97

Z…..K

Good grief. It was not the most stimulating work I've ever done, so I looked for something else to do to stay creative. That's what I do. I can't sit still for long. I've got to keep moving, keep going forward.

It was time to start work on getting that voice-over career going here in my new city. That was the ultimate goal in moving to L.A., so let's have at it. That meant working on it at least one hour a day but I had no idea where to start. I needed to get in touch with all the ad agencies in town but I didn't know where to find that list. Then I realized every single audiotape that came into KHTZ with commercials had the name of the ad agency and the studio where the commercials were recorded right on the label. Whenever a new box was delivered, I wrote down the names, then sent whatever agency it was my own demo tape with a note to introduce myself, then a follow-up card one week later. I wrote letters to every voice-over agent in L.A. I did most of the work at home before my shift, then made copies of my demo tape later that night when I got off the air. I dragged a typewriter into the studio to print address labels for my demo boxes. I was relentless.

Gradually, I started to make some headway in voice-overs. I got an agent from all the submissions I sent, and started to book a few jobs here and there. By the spring of 1982, I got a big break. Jim Gibbons owned a company called Flamingo Films and he did movie trailers. At that time he was working on the TV and radio commercials for a little film called "Fast Times at Ridgemont High." It was a teen movie that turned into a somewhat iconic film, launching the careers of Sean Penn, Cameron Crowe, and Amy Heckerling. Jim put me on everything, the trailer, television commercials, and radio spots. It was a real thrill, my first big voice-

over gig. I was booked a few times a week to record voice track after voice track, change after change. I was surprised by how much work went into this and by how well it paid. The movie was released in August of '82 and I made enough money to bank for the future and also refurbish my little red Niki Lauda, Alfa Romeo convertible sports car. A total win-win.

Also during this time, the nine p.m. shift opened up at the station and I told Stoney he should send in his aircheck. About three months after Ann and I had moved to Los Angeles, Stoney and Barbara came out, too. Neither one of them had any work lined up and it was tough going for a while. Stoney took any job he could find while he pursued his acting career. He drove a truck for the Department of Water and Power for a few weeks, and he worked as a bar-back at the Palomino in the San Fernando Valley. When I heard about the opening at KHTZ, I made sure he sent me his demo and then I walked it into the PD's office. I said, "You gotta hear this guy," and by the end of the week, Stoney got the job. Our shifts had flipped since we first met. Instead of me following him as I did at WKYS, he followed me every night at nine p.m. To his credit, Stoney was NEVER late.

By now, two years had gone by since we moved to L.A. Earlier, I know I complained about the format at KHTZ and how strict everything was, but I had grown up enough to know that job was a great opportunity. Now it was time to negotiate a new contract with the station and I was ready to take another risk. I had toyed with the idea of moving full time into voice-overs, but the realist in me knew I needed to continue with radio as my "day job." Meanwhile, Ann had found a job she loved at KABC-TV. She was writing the news and producing mini-documentaries for the

six and eleven o'clock newscasts, surrounded by smart, creative reporters, camera operators, and editors. She was inspired by the work, and making a great salary. I was happy for her and relieved she had a good job. That was the atmosphere at home when I entered into contract talks with the general manager at KHTZ, an all-around nice guy named Bob Moore. The station was doing pretty well, nothing like the successes of WKYS and Q107, but respectable. I hoped to start making up for the pay cut I took when I came to L.A. When I asked Bob for a pay raise, he told me there just wasn't any more money in the budget. Whatever I made in the previous year was what I was going to get the next year, take it or leave it. Finally he said, "And furthermore, if you can't DOUBLE what I'm paying you on those voice-overs you're doing, you should just pack up and go back to D.C."

We agreed to disagree. Here I was, making the same decision my friend Stoney had made a few years earlier when he walked away from Q107. Should I give up my full-time job to gamble on a freelance career, just like he did to find work as an actor? My voice-over income was nowhere near what I could make in radio but I still decided to resign from the station. When I found out I wasn't getting that raise, I felt as if I had stopped moving forward. I needed to keep some momentum going with voice-overs despite the risk of giving up a full-time job. Annie's paycheck would have to pay the bills for a while.

The management at KHTZ was actually very nice and gave me a Saturday night shift to keep me going while I figured out what to do next. To this day, whenever I bump into Bob Moore at party or event in town, he always says to anyone within earshot, "I am the one that gave Joe Cipriano his voice-over career. I

told him he could double the money I was paying him, so if it weren't for me, Cipriano would never have done promos." He loves telling that story and I get a good laugh out of it, too.

My life slowed down considerably when I gave up my full-time shift for weekends. Once again, I didn't have a job only this time I did it to myself. I spent every day sending out voice-over demos and radio airchecks to stations in L.A. looking for a new gig, but nothing happened. I started to feel like I had made the worst choice of my life. Then, out of the blue, I got lucky.

This might be a good time to talk about those accidental, serendipitous moments most of us call luck. It's happened to me quite a few times in my life. Like when a nine-year-old kid, on a random field trip, saw a couple of grownups clowning around at work on the radio, or when a young teenage boy called a radio station to talk to the deejay and he turned out to be a nice guy, or when a happy-go-lucky fella bumped into the right girl at the right time in an empty hallway. I am always looking for luck.

Sometimes luck can hit you so hard it knocks you down like a landslide, impossible to miss. Other times, it can be as soft as a whisper, floating by unnoticed. The trick is to pay attention. You have to be ready to jump on those opportunities. The chance of a lifetime could be right in front of you, but unless you're prepared to meet it halfway, it might just slide by. I try to always keep working on my skills so I'm ready to take advantage of those special moments. I think of it almost like striking a matchstick. You need to ignite that spark so it catches fire. I even believe there are certain times of the year that are luckier for me than other times. Unfortunately there are also those days that have traditionally been unlucky. I look forward with anticipation for

the good days, and hunker down for the bad. If I can get through the crappy days without incident, I always breathe a huge sigh of relief.

I will never forget some advice I got from an acting teacher here in Los Angeles. His name was Wayne Dvorak. He said people always ask him why some actors make it, and others don't. His answer was beautiful. He believed when you work towards your dream, a little red light glows on top of your head. When you stop working, or get distracted, that light dims, or goes off completely. He said it's important to keep that light glowing because the Gods of Making Dreams Come True are sitting up in the cosmos looking for those bright lights. They want to help make your dream come true. You've got to keep working at it, keep looking for luck, so it can find you to help you reach your goal.

Now there I was, on a Saturday night, saying, "K-H-T-Z…K-HITS-97," when the hot line rang, and a job fell into my lap. Remember, this was 1983, before cell phones. I picked it up, "Yello?"

"Dave?"

"Yeah, it's Dave. Who is this?" I didn't recognize the voice but figured it must be someone from Connecticut since he didn't call me Joe.

"Dave, it's Ed Scarborough, you might remember me as Ed Mitchell at WDRC in Hartford."

DRC is where I used the name Dave Donovan.

"Ed, wow…how the heck are you doing, we haven't talked in eight years."

"Yeah, I know, but I think you'll be happy to hear from me."

I laughed and said, "Of course I'm happy to hear from you."

He said, "You don't know the half of it. Dave, I'm programming KHTR in St. Louis."

St. Louis? I didn't like where this was going.

"But I'm leaving the station and I'm coming to Los Angeles. I'm the new program director of the CBS FM station there. It's called KNX-FM."

I was familiar with KNX. It was a soft album station.

"Dave, we're changing it to KKHR HIT RADIO 93. We're going to be a high-energy Hot Hits station and I'm wondering if you might be interested in a job."

I tried not to gush, but I think I blurted out, "Hell yeah."

"Great, but listen, couple of incidentals, send me an aircheck I can play for my bosses."

"No problem."

"Oh, and would you mind using the name Dave Donovan again? I loved that name when you were at WDRC and would really like you to use it again."

Dave, Joe, Tommy? I didn't care. He could have called me anything he wanted to, it would have been fine with me. Just as Doug Limerick, Al Brady Law, and so many others saved my radio life in D.C., Ed Scarborough dug me out of the ground here in L.A. He put together a solid team. Lou Simon did the morning show, I was hired for early middays, nine a.m. to noon,

followed by Chris Lance, Todd Parker in afternoons, and Dancin'
Mark Hanson from six to midnight. It was a formulaic format
that worked on several CBS FM stations around the country,
extremely high energy, with reverb on the microphone and a
tight Hot Hit rotation of 30 songs. It was going to be the next big
thing to take over Los Angeles, except it wasn't.

In my opinion, CBS announced its plan way too soon, two
months before the changeover. KIIS-FM was already playing a
Top 40 format in Los Angeles, with a talented morning man, but
the station was floundering around the middle of the ratings pile,
when its Program Director Gerry DeFrancesco heard what CBS
was up to. He decided he'd beat us to the punch. It was a brilliant
move. He made a deal with Mike Joseph, who had once tried to
hire me in Providence, Rhode Island. Joseph owned the rights to
the slogan "Hot Hits," and KIIS-FM licensed it before CBS had
locked it up. Then KIIS handed the morning show keys and carte
blanche to their talented morning man named Rick Dees and
cranked up the volume. That was bad enough for KKHR, but on
top of that, going against all expectations, for some reason CBS
wouldn't put any money into promoting our station. When we
went on the air that summer in 1983, we were like lambs led to
the slaughter.

KKHR's sound was exciting, energetic, and fun but nobody
heard us. We gave away turkeys at Thanksgiving. Yes, dead, frozen
turkeys. KIIS-FM gave away a Porsche 911. Not just one, but they
gave away one Porsche every week. Oh, and they stuffed ten $100
bills in the glove box of each car. That's what we were up against.

Against those odds, I still had a great time. Personally, my life
couldn't have been better. Ann and I had bought our first home

in the Palisades. It was barely 900 square feet and cost almost $200,000. We could walk one way down the street into town, or turn the other way and walk to the ocean. And we were about to become one of those parents pushing a stroller down the sidewalk. Ann was pregnant for the first time. Our daughter Dayna was born while I worked at KKHR.

As far as work was concerned, I gave KKHR my best shot, we all did, but it didn't last long. When the ratings came out, KIIS went into double digits with a ten share, and we had a four. Ed Scarborough was under terrible pressure to make something happen. Amazingly, we kept it going for about two years, but CBS wasn't happy with the ratings. I soon found out the executives back east weren't happy with the nine to noon guy either. That was me. One of the programming vice presidents at CBS Black Rock in New York just hated my voice. He repeatedly told Ed to get rid of me until finally in June of 1985, Ed had to let me go. I guess I knew it was coming but it still hurt. Fired for the second time in my life, only now I had a wife, and baby. Without even thinking twice about it, I walked out of that meeting, down the hall to the jock lounge, picked up the phone and called Gerry DeFrancesco at KIIS.

"Gerry, KKHR is letting me go. Do you have anything for me, even weekends?"

Gerry said, "Joe, I love what you do, love your voice, you belong over here. I've got something on the AM station. It's not KIIS-FM but it pays the same, probably more than you're making at KKHR."

"When can I start?"

"C'mon over tomorrow. We'll get you set up and I'll introduce you to everybody. I'll put you on the overnight shift so you can get started, then move you to the ten p.m. spot."

Earlier that day, Dave Donovan went on the air at KKHR. Tomorrow Joe Cipriano would come back to life, this time on KIIS-AM. How strange.

KIIS AM & FM

The biggest, big-time station I have ever worked at was KIIS radio. Number one in Los Angeles. It was huge! The FM that is, not exactly where I was going. The AM was number 25 in the ratings. At that time, there was a rule by the FCC that prohibited major market stations from simulcasting on both AM and FM. We played the same music as the FM, the same commercials, even the same jingles, but we had a completely different on-air staff. And when I say we played the same music, I mean we played the exact same song at the exact same time. KIIS was allowed to simulcast Rick Dees from six in the morning until ten, after that the two stations parted ways. On the AM, Steve Lehman did middays, Larry Morgan afternoons, Benny Martinez was on from six to ten at night, then I came on from ten to two in the morning, followed by Tom Murphy on the overnight shift.

Listen, it was a job and it paid good money, but if I thought we didn't have a big audience on KKHR, we had next to no one listening on KIIS-AM. I hadn't worked on an AM station since WWCO, and that was ten years ago. KIIS-AM had a point one share. Not a one share, a POINT one. I would do a contest to give away an album or concert tickets, to the twentieth caller, and it turned out the winner had also been the fifth caller, and the eleventh, and the fifteenth, before we both finally hit number 20. Sometimes it seemed there were more people listening to the station in our building than there were out in the entire city.

Since absolutely no one was paying attention to us, we tried to amuse ourselves. My friend, comedy writer Louise Palanker, who wrote the Rick Dees Weekly Top 40 show, liked to work at night. With her at the station most evenings, I would utilize her comedic skills for a "joke-off" bit I did. Weeze, as I called her, would tell a joke on the air and one of our phone operators at the station would tell a joke and we let our four listeners decide who won. Weeze and I shared many late-night laughs and talks about our futures.

With my whole day free I worked even harder on jump-starting my voice-over career. I discovered that finding work in this business is a never-ending quest. Unless you're in such demand that you actually have to turn down a job, you need to stay on top of what's happening around you. That's where a good agent comes into play. By this time, I had already been represented by Nina Nisenholtz at the iconic William Morris Agency. The building was one block over from Rodeo Drive in Beverly Hills. It was a thrill going into the office for auditions, even if I didn't book a gig that week. Later I worked with Vanessa Gilbert at TGI and then Steve Tisherman. But I found my true home with an Italian girl, Rita Vennari. I have been with Rita at Sutton, Barth, and Vennari for over 20 years. Agents Mary Ellen Lord and Jessica Bulavsky are my right and left hands at SBV. Together Rita, Mary Ellen, and Jessica helped me reinvent myself several times over as I started to land a couple of great jobs.

After doing "Fast Times at Ridgemont High," I was booked to do some commercials and trailers for other teen movies like "Porky's," "Bachelor Party," and a Tom Cruise movie called "All the Right Moves." I started doing a few spots for a TV show called "Scarecrow and Mrs. King," and voiced the intro of the "Bugs Bunny and Tweety Show" every Saturday morning on ABC. I even booked a national on-camera commercial for Prego

Spaghetti Sauce. I was flown to New York, first class, for the shoot and while I was there I snuck up to Connecticut to see my family.

Even with all of that going on, it wasn't enough to support my family. After Dayna was born, Ann went back to work at KABC-TV and ended up on a local afternoon talk show with the iconic newsman Tom Snyder. Most people remember Tom from the "Tomorrow Show," in the seventies and eighties. Or from Dan Aykroyd's hilarious imitation of Tom on "Saturday Night Live." Tom was a blast, a real original. He liked to say, "I used to be coast to coast. Now I'm freeway to freeway." It turned out to be the best time Ann ever had on a job. She worked with a wonderful group of women, Debbie Alpert, Bonnie Tiegel, Claudia Martin, and Lois Spieler. I was relieved she loved that job because we really needed her salary. One night I was at KIIS-AM, chatting with Louise, when I admitted, "Weeze, you're catching me at the lowest point in my radio career." Later she told me how shocked she was to hear what I had said. She thought I was the most upbeat, centered, happy person she had ever met and here I was blurting out that I was hitting bottom. Then, wouldn't you know it, more bad luck.

About a year into my show at KIIS-AM, I was at work on the night shift when I heard the bell go off on that damn AP machine again. At least it wasn't a bulletin this time, only a news alert. I ripped the story from the machine and realized it was worse than I thought. The FCC had just ruled to remove those restrictions against simulcasting in major markets. I blinked, then read the story again. I knew what it meant. KIIS would now be able to simulcast the AM and FM stations. The AM on-air staff would be let go immediately. That little innocuous blurb meant I was out of work, again.

We had two weeks before the changeover. I'll never forget one particular night during that time, before my shift. I walked into the FM studio to say hello to the very talented Tim Kelly

who was on the air. I used to listen to him on Super CFL out of Chicago when I was back in Connecticut. Despite the pending disaster, I was the same guy I always was, so first I joked around with the phone operators before going into the studio. I might even have been laughing at something when I opened the door to see Tim. I can picture him right now. He looked up at me from the control board and said, "Why are you so fucking happy? You just lost your job and you've got another kid on the way?"

Yep, number two baby comin' atcha. I didn't know what to say to him. I don't think Tim meant it to hurt as much as it did, but it hit me right in the kisser. I probably mumbled something like, "We'll be okay. I've just gotta give it time." I don't know what I said. What could I say?

My last night on KIIS-AM I threw a party. I was determined to have an on-air blowout. Most of the jocks had already jumped ship but I had nowhere to go. With hardly anyone left on staff, I went on the air as usual, at ten o'clock, and stayed until midnight. I invited everyone to stop by, brought in beer, and ordered a bunch of pizzas. The AM station was under the same old regulation that forced us to drop the power down to next to nothing at sundown. But tonight I said screw it. When I went on the air at ten, the first thing I did was crank that transmitter up to full power. Then I threw out the format and played whatever the hell I wanted to play. Ron Shapiro was the production genius at the station and he recorded the entire show, not only just what went out over the airwaves, but what we said in the studio too, when the microphones were turned off. We kept within the FCC rules, no cursing or swearing, but it was outrageous. Steve Lehman came by with his wife Suzie, Bruce Vidal, Bumpy Woods, Larry Morgan, Tom Murphy, Ed Mann, Benny Martinez, Louise Palanker, and Tim Kelly. I'm proud I was a part of that last show on KIIS-AM. It was by far our most entertaining show ever.

At the end of my shift, as we closed in on midnight, I loaded up every cart machine with our name jingles, for all the jocks, then played them all in a row, one after the other. "Joe Cipriano… KIIS AMmmmmmmm." It was a roll call of all the on-air staff. When the last one played, I let about ten seconds of silence go by, then flipped the switch for the FM signal to take over. That was the end of KIIS-AM.

It was 1987. I was down, but I wasn't out, not yet. There was still a little radio life left in me. Gerry DeFran had one lonely shift left open on the FM if I wanted it, Sunday morning, the overnight, from three a.m. until nine a.m. "Gulp, how the mediocre have fallen," I thought. Not exactly prime time but it was a job. I went from full-time to part-time, again. I was pullin' in one hundred seventy dollars…a week. Wait a minute. That's what I made back in Connecticut when I was 19 years old and worked at WWCO. Only this was Los Angeles! Welcome to major-market radio. Thankfully, Ann saved us again. "The Tom Snyder Show" had been canceled to make room for an unknown personality from Chicago, Oprah Winfrey. If her show didn't make it, her boss promised to bring back Tom. I guess we know how that went. Fortunately, Ann found a gig working on "Lifestyles of the Rich and Famous." Remember Robin Leach? "Champagne wishes and caviar dreams!" She was making big bucks now as a member of the Directors Guild union, but our second child was due in June, so I had to come up with something fast, while she took maternity leave.

I kept that three in the morning shift, and little by little started to produce promos for KIIS-FM, working in the production room about four days a week. Gerry DeFran had moved on to another station and our new PD Steve Rivers liked me. He started to use me as a fill-in guy. Whenever a jock took time off, I took over that shift. A few days producing and voicing promos for KIIS-FM,

a few days of on-air fill-in and all of those bits and pieces added up to a five- or-six day work week. Soon I was back up to a full-time salary. Man, did we need that help because our son, Alex, was born two months early.

I was able to make it work at KIIS-FM for another full year. There were a couple of months where I did the night shift from ten until two in the morning, alternating with Benny Martinez. One week on, one week off while the programming geniuses tried to decide who should get the job permanently. It ended up neither one of us got the gig, they gave it to somebody else. I kept filling in here and there, plus I still produced promos and commercials for the station. Rick Dees was huge, number one in the ratings, and he always gave me encouragement. When I voiced a promo, he'd send me a note telling me how good I sounded. If I produced a promo that he voiced, he sent me another encouraging note. He didn't have to do any of that, but he always gave me reinforcement and a little bit of hope. The bottom line was, that I was at the number one station in Los Angeles. Even if I wasn't on the air full-time, I was part of a team of great people. It was enough to pay our mortgage and keep food on the table. I still loved my job, still tried to move forward. I had a great voice-over agent, worked on my demos, got some bookings and kept my eyes open for that elusive spark to catch fire. I was looking to get lucky. And then it happened.

I was filling in for Big Ron O'Brien on KIIS-FM, doing his afternoon shift while he was on vacation, when I got an unexpected phone call. That call would lead to a whole new opportunity. My big break. It would take me completely out of radio and into the world of promo.

My last job as a disc jockey was at KIIS-FM.

My first job as a network promo voice was at FOX television.

You can't get much luckier than that.

THREE BEEPS

"It's an all-new Simpsons on Fox!"

Those seven little words changed my life.

I was a part-time disc jockey at KIIS-FM radio in Los Angeles when this guy called me out of the blue and handed me the opportunity of a lifetime. It was summertime, 1988 and I was filling in for Big Ron O'Brien on the afternoon shift, from two to six p.m. That was prime-time radio on the number one station in town. Even if it was just for one week, I was one happy guy. Meanwhile, I had no idea there was this other guy, a network executive, stuck in traffic on the San Diego Freeway trying to get home from his job in Hollywood, way out to Simi Valley. That's a long commute, even on a good day, and that particular day, traffic was bad. The only company he had with him in the car was me, on the radio. With my voice as his backdrop he fixated on a problem he was having at work. He had recently been hired by a brand-new television network called FOX. It was only on the air a couple of nights a week and his job was to try to get TV viewers to change the channel from one of the Big Three networks to the new one. It's hard to get people to change their viewing habits but he was smart, talented, and very determined. Together with his partner they were the golden boys of marketing. They had been over at NBC when FOX lured them

away. Their job was to find an image for FOX that sounded like what the network looked like, new, young, and exciting.

I must have been having a good day because listening to me on the radio that afternoon, he suddenly thought, "Now that's a voice that could work for FOX." There was that certain something about me that clicked for him. He felt I sounded youthful, warm, enthusiastic, like a guy just out of college, filled with anticipation for the future. He couldn't have been closer to the truth, except for that college thing. He thought I sounded like the kind of person you'd like to invite over to your house for dinner. He picked up his brick of a 1988 cell phone and dialed KIIS-FM. The receptionist buzzed me in the studio. I remember the call coming in that day. I asked her to give the guy my agent's name and number and figured, "Cool. This could be a new spot for me to voice." My agent set up an audition and that's when I met him.

His name was Bob Bibb and his partner was Lewis Goldstein. They were the heads of on-air promotion for FOX television. Together, those two men would launch my career to places I didn't even know existed. That opportunity turned out to be my golden gig. I started doing television promos for the FOX network and I never looked back. The crazy thing about the way I landed that gig? I wasn't even supposed to be on the radio that day. I was just filling in.

When I went to audition for Bob and Lew, they had me voice promos for "The Joan Rivers Show," then spots for "The Tracy Ullman Show," and also the upcoming Emmy awards. FOX was broadcasting the Emmys that year, scheduled to air at the end of August. It's always a big deal for any network to present the Emmy show, but especially for FOX because it wasn't even a full-time network yet. It was still less than one year old. None

of its shows were even nominated for an Emmy and here it was, responsible for presenting the show that celebrated the best of all that television had to offer.

I don't remember exactly how many promos FOX produced for that one night of programming, but there must have been over 100. Bob put me on every single one. I made more money that month doing promos for the Emmy show than I would have made in an entire year as a disc jockey at KIIS-FM. There was one night when I read 20 spots and 60 tags. A "spot" is the same thing as a promo, just a different name. It could be any length of time: 30 seconds, 20 seconds, even ten or 15 seconds. A "tag" is the update of the promo. On a tag, you might only have to say "tonight," "tomorrow," or "next." In SAG/AFTRA, my union, the voice-over talent is paid by the "spot and tag." Twenty spots are roughly $4,300, a little more than two hundred dollars each. Sixty tags are $5,500, a little less than one hundred dollars each. That one session equaled almost $10,000. Jackpot! It was beyond belief.

The Emmys did fairly well on FOX that year and soon I was doing all the comedy promos at FOX: "Married...with Children," "The Tracy Ullman Show," a show called "Duet," and the longest-running show of them all, "The Simpsons." Bob and Lew hired another guy to voice all the dramas. Maybe you know him? His name is Don LaFontaine. Even if you haven't heard of him, you have definitely heard his voice. He was the most sought-after voice-over artist in the business. I saw Don nearly every day over the next few years. He would go into one audio room, I was in another. We would switch rooms to work with different producers, then flip back again. The pace was fast and furious.

Doing promos for television had been my goal ever since we moved to Los Angeles. For the first time ever I felt like I

was really a part of show business. I found myself totally invested into the notion that whatever the particular show was that I was promoting at that moment must be the best show on television. I wasn't lying to myself. I bought into it. I was completely immersed in the characters, the premise, the plot, and the jokes of every program I voiced. I also believed any show I was promoting was the result of a lot of very talented people putting all they had into their work, and I was determined to do that as well. I didn't want to let anyone down.

I learned a lot about promos from Bob and Lew. They are extremely creative and absolute perfectionists, so much so, that you can find as many people who love them as loathe them. They are also workaholics and expect everyone else to work as hard as they do. I'll always remember one Mother's Day when I had planned a nice weekend for Ann, with our kids, Dayna and Alex. FOX was in the middle of something called "upfronts." That's when the networks create special two-minute presentations of all the most popular shows on TV, and also showcase their new programs. It happens every May and it's how the networks entice advertisers to buy commercials for the upcoming fall season. Everything is on the line for the TV executives and it's always a tense, frenetic pace of activity. Those two-minute promos are worked, reworked, and reread many times over until they are perfect, before they are presented at the upfronts.

I was at FOX on Friday, still a week away from the upfront presentations, and Lew said, "We need you on Sunday to voice some of this stuff." I said, "Lew, I'm taking Ann and the kids to Santa Barbara for the weekend to celebrate Mother's Day." He said, "OK, we'll do it later in the day." I said, "Well, we're going to be up there all day, on the beach relaxing."

To his credit, he was willing to work with me. Lew said, "All right, we won't book you until nighttime."

This was my first experience with upfronts. I had no idea what went into it and I looked at him like he was crazy, saying, "Lew I'm out of town."

Finally he blurted out, "Son of a bitch, Joe, it's Mother's DAY, not Mother's NIGHT!"

It was so outrageous, I could only laugh, but finally, I realized what the hell was going on. This was not radio anymore. This was television and this was BIG. Millions of dollars BIG. I got back in plenty of time on Sunday night to get the job done.

I have to say, this was one of the most exciting times of my career. Everything seemed to be going my way. One month before the upfronts, I was cast in a sitcom for NBC, called "Knight and Daye" and starring Jack Warden, Mason Adams, and Julia Campbell. It was set in a fictional radio station in San Diego where Warden and Adams were brought back together by program director Campbell to recreate their successful 1950s radio team which they called Knight and Daye. I played the deejay on the air before them, Marty in the Morning. It was a summer series and we were given the perfect lead-in. Our little sitcom was going to follow the most popular show on television, "The Cosby Show."

Good god, I thought, this was going to change my career once again. I started dreaming that in no time at all I would move from off-camera to on-camera in an NBC sitcom of my own, starring Joe Cipriano. My first day on the set the news got even better. The pilot episode of "Knight and Daye" would be directed by the very talented Bill Persky, one of the writers of the classic "Dick Van Dyke Show." Just as exciting for me, Persky was the writer/

producer of "Good Morning World," the TV show that inspired my last-minute dashes into work back when I was at WKYS in Washington. The A-list talent pool didn't stop there. The creators and writers of the show were Babaloo Mandell and Lowell Ganz. They were nearly invincible after writing successful movies like "City Slickers," "Parenthood," "Splash," their list goes on and on. We hit the air with huge expectations and then the ratings came out. For whatever reason, it just didn't work. "Knight and Daye" lasted about seven episodes before NBC pulled the plug. So much for my sitcom career.

Okay, I wasn't going to be the next big TV star but I still had FOX promos. And I was determined to be the best damn promo voice I could be. Whenever I read a promo, I thoroughly enjoy it. During a spot, you usually read an opening line, such as "Sunday on the Simpsons…" then you stop and there is sound up from one of the characters from the show playing out a scene. Many times these are some of the best jokes in the entire episode and I usually react to it and laugh along. That's why many people have told me that I have a genuine enthusiasm and excitement about the shows I'm promoting. That I sound as if I'm smiling all the time. Busted. It's true. I won't say that I'm an easy laugh. I just take pleasure in and appreciate the effort to entertain me as well as the rest of the audience. Because of that, I'm able to add a truly believable vibe to my work. I find that if you jump in and get involved rather than stand back and scrutinize, the results are more positive.

Reading a promo reminds me of talking up an intro of a song from my radio days. It was a natural transition that lined up perfectly with my skills as a disc jockey. When you get ready to read a spot, you pop on your headphones, and in your ears you

hear three separate beeps, then silence. On the imaginary fourth beep, that's when you start reading the script. Three beeps, then GO. Timing is important, understanding how to "sell" the product is important, sounding like you're NOT selling the product is even more important. It's about believing in what you're saying and genuinely having a good time while you're doing it.

Quality and speed are also necessary for a promo voice to be successful. In my line of work as a deejay, I could talk up the intro of a song on the radio to the last fraction of a second before the vocal hit. In promos, the measurement of time is in frames. There are 30 frames in one second. We leave ten frames at the end of a promo so the last letter of the last word doesn't get chopped off. In the first take, if I leave only eight frames, you better believe I'll give them ten frames in take two.

Working at FOX was my first experience at a television network. Sure, I had jobs at NBC and ABC, but those were radio gigs. This was different. I was surprised by a couple of things. First, nearly everyone who worked there was young, in their twenties or thirties. And second, for such a young staff, they were extraordinary. That's what FOX had going for it. Everyone was bright, willing to try something new, anxious to do the best job possible. It was a true collaboration that started from the top.

I remember the first time I met our new head of advertising and promotions, Sandy Grushow. It was the summer of 1988 and he had just come over to television from the feature film division of FOX. I went to see him at his new office. He welcomed me warmly and literally rolled up his sleeves as he asked me to help him rewrite a promo he was working on. He's that kind of guy. He gets down in the trenches with his people. Of course, he also knew how to play the corporate game with his peers, but even in

his suit he came across as a regular guy, just like the rest of us. It wasn't long before Sandy was promoted all the way to the top at 32 years of age, making him the youngest executive to ever hold the title of network president.

That was the atmosphere at FOX, loose, energetic, filled with extraordinary people. From the scheduling staff upstairs, like Senior Vice President Steve Weinheimer, to the audio room producers like Susan Berman, Alison Bloom, Grace Cowper, Phil Ohler and Rob Lawe, each person did their job professionally, quickly, to perfection. It was a thrill to go to work every day. When Bob and Lew moved on, Geoff Calnan replaced them, another gifted, marketing genius. Over the years, Geoff has become one of my dearest friends and his creative brilliance glows brightly to this day. He is a true renaissance man. I think he can do just about anything.

There was a multitude of talent at FOX, but without a doubt, one of the best and brightest of all was Ron Scalera. He joined Bob Bouknight, another young, exceptional marketing talent who was already on board. As the network grew, we did too, and along the way I got to know both of them quite well, especially Ron.

Born in New Jersey, Ron Scalera had worked in New York before moving out west. Both of us were from the East Coast, both of us had an Italian upbringing, and both of us had a love for television from the time we were kids. We hit it off right away. He started out writing and producing promos, but it was obvious from the start that there was something special about Ron. He knew exactly what he wanted in a spot from the beginning. He was able to visualize how the promo would look and sound before he ever cut anything. It was like a golfer who visualizes his shot before he hits it. He sees the flight of the ball and knows where it will land, then makes it happen when he hits the ball. Ron knew

what the end result would be before he even started.

As a director of voice talent, Ron also knew precisely what he wanted from his voice-over people. I can't tell you how wonderful that is for someone in my position. I didn't mind doing multiple takes on a read for Ron, because he knew how to get you to where you needed to be, and when you got there, he was done, no more takes. This sounds simple, but there are many very creative people who don't have that vision. For them, it's more of an "I'll know it when I hear it" sort of thing. That means you end up throwing a bunch of different reads up against the studio glass until they hear something that works. It can be frustrating and lead to tempers flaring up and voices going hoarse. Ron may have had you read a bunch of times, but you knew where you were going and trusted him completely.

Bob and Lew quickly saw that Ron was a superstar. They had him produce huge image pieces for the network and ultimately Ron was put in charge of creative imaging for the entire FOX television network under Sandy's guidance. With that kind of reputation, it wasn't long before Ron was hired away to work for someone else. CBS President Leslie Moonves had heard about Ron Scalera and wanted him for his own. It happened in June of 1997. We had nearly nine years together at FOX and had forged a lasting friendship. Once he settled into his new job at CBS he pulled me into the fold to voice comedies at that network, too.

I don't know anyone who didn't like Ron. He was joy multiplied ten thousand times. He loved music, television, smoking cigars, drinking good scotch, his friends, and most of all, his family, back in Jersey and here in Los Angeles. Ron's wife, Elizabeth, is from Maryland, like Ann, so we had that in common, too. And they have two wonderful kids, Rachel and Michael.

I spent a fair amount of time with Ron just talking about life. A group of us joined the Grand Havana Room cigar club in Beverly Hills and shared a box filled with stogies. That box had a gold nameplate on it that read "FOX," then after Ron moved to CBS, we renamed it "Monkey." Ron said, "You can't say 'monkey' without smiling." It's still there today. Our Grand Havana Room group includes Ron Mulligan, Mark and Chris Bonn, Paul Robie and one of Ron's closest buddies, Bob Campbell. Thinking about those nights makes my heart heavy because Ron left us way too soon.

The last time I saw him alive, Ann and I were at his house for a night of tennis. Elizabeth had invited me to play with some of her friends. Ann and Ron sat back to watch us run around the court and to catch up on their lives. They talked about our kids, what they were doing and where they were going. It was a beautiful evening. We made plans to do it again soon, but a few days later I got the horrible news.

It was April 21, 2010, and Ron was getting ready to go back east to see his family in Jersey. His brother was very sick and Ron wasn't sure if this trip might be the last time he would see his brother alive. It was early that morning and he was taking his dog out for a walk before heading to the airport when he collapsed in the street. There were people around who rushed to help him. In fact, we heard that one of the first to get to Ron's side was actor Matt LeBlanc from the TV show "Friends." LeBlanc was in the neighborhood when he saw Ron fall to the ground, but it was already too late. Ron was gone in an instant. He was 49 years old.

Ron was unlike anyone I had ever met before. He was the ultimate feel-good fun guy. He wanted everyone to have the best time possible and he took us all on the ride of our lives.

He organized different outings, golf weekends, eating weekends, anything that would bring his friends together. We did cigar mixers, scotch mixers, mixer mixers, then woke up the next morning to play golf and drink some more. He played the guitar in a band with Paul Robie, and Brian Dollenmeyer, at that time the new head of marketing at FOX. We were always in the front row at the Canyon Club in Camarillo to listen to and dance to their music. The look on Ron's face while he sang and played his guitar was pure happiness.

One night, Ron and Elizabeth, Paul and Michelle Robie were over for dinner. We were living in Beverly Hills at that time, in a beautiful Mediterranean home with a pool and a tennis court. Ron said, "Joey, I know you love tennis. Let's go hit some balls on your court." We went outside, me hitting against Paulie and Ron, each of them holding a tumbler of scotch on the rocks in one hand and a tennis racket in the other.

Ron pulled CBS up by the bootstraps and grabbed it around the nape of its neck to help it become the number one network in television. Les Moonves did his magic with the programming, but Ron created campaigns that made people watch. He "got them into the tent" as the saying goes. I don't even know if the regular TV viewer knew why he needed to turn on CBS at eight p.m. every night, but he did it because Ron Scalera told him so.

I can't believe how much I miss him and I'll never be able to thank him enough for what he did for me. I wouldn't be where I am today without Ron. You don't always get to be friends with the people you work with, but that's happened for me many times over again. Ron, Susan Berman Moore, Geoff Calnan, Garen van de Beek and going back a few years, Stoney Richards, and Barbara Grieco. So many people. I think it comes from being

open, helpful, willing to do whatever it takes to get the job done right. People notice that kind of work ethic and it isn't always the boss in charge. Most times, it's your co-workers who appreciate the effort you take to make something they are working on even better.

Remember the first time I met Willard Scott at NBC in Washington, back in 1975? He grabbed me in a bear hug then planted a big wet kiss on my forehead. He greeted every single person with a smile. I never forgot that. I wanted to be the same kind of guy. I wanted to be one of the high points of someone's day, not the low point. Besides, most of what I do only takes about 15 minutes a session. But the engineer, the writer, the editor, chances are those people are working an eight-hour shift, sometimes more. I was not going to come into the room complaining about my day.

I love my job, but honestly it's the personal relationships that mean so much to me. Those friendships might not pay the bills but they have enriched my life in ways that money can't buy. Those are the people who inspire you to do better, to reach higher. And you're about to meet two of the best.

DON AND DANNY

Years ago I was out to dinner with a bunch of voice-over people, Joan Baker, George DelHoyo, Sylvia Villagran, plus a few other friends. The man sitting next to me looked at the menu, then leaned over and in the voice that launched a million blockbusters, he said, "We should get the caviar tonight, for an appetizer." I nearly gagged when I saw the price. It was $320 for some ridiculously small amount. I said, "No way, it's too expensive." He looked at me with a grin then said, "Joey, it's a spot and a tag!"

That man was the late, great Don LaFontaine. Of course, we got the caviar.

I've already told you a little bit about Don when we worked together at FOX. He is probably the most successful voice-over artist of all time. Don passed away in 2008 yet he still holds the record for the most contracts ever filed by the Screen Actors Guild. He recorded hundreds of thousands of spots to promote movies, television shows, radio stations, commercial products, anything and everything. Then there was the television commercial he did for the Geico Insurance Company. That's the one where you actually got to see what he looked like, on camera. Don was second to no one. He even inspired a movie, a comedy about the people who work in voice-over, called "In A World," written, directed by, and starring the extremely talented Lake Bell. I have

a small part in the movie, playing myself in a couple of scenes. Once you see what Don meant to our industry, you'll understand why producers loved and feared him. Agents courted him. Up-and-comers tried to sound like him. All of us respected him.

Don was already a legend when I met him for the first time. It was at a studio in Los Angeles on Third Street, just east of Fairfax, in 1982, way before the FOX network was created. I was at the studio to voice a trailer for "Fast Times at Ridgemont High." When I walked into the room, the producer told me they weren't quite ready yet, so he asked me to take a seat. The lights were low but I could see there was a man sitting in a dark corner, looking down at a book on his lap. The producer called out for someone to get a cup of coffee for Cipriano, and that's when this guy looked up and said, "Cipriano? Are you Joe?"

I was blown away by that voice. It sounded like it was coming out of a speaker. Crisp, clean, clear, and deep. Even though we had never met before, I knew exactly who it was.

"Yeah, I'm Joe." I smiled back, happy to finally meet the "Voice of God."

"I've heard you on some stuff. You're pretty good, kid."

"Thanks! I'm a big fan of yours."

"Yeah, everyone is," he cracked back. That was Don. Funny, self-deprecating, brilliant.

I reached out to shake hands and when he stood up I got my first look at the famous Don. About my height, he had on a black satin shirt, open to the middle of his chest, with a thick gold chain hanging from his neck. I noticed a big watch on his wrist and an even bigger buckle on the belt stretched around his ample waist. I had already heard Don wore a toupee, and there it was, a

dark, curly hairpiece sitting on top of his head. When he turned to sit back down I saw a huge falcon or some other monster bird embroidered on the back of his shirt. Now I knew who owned the muscle car sitting out by the front door in the parking lot. I used to think Don dressed to match his various cars. With a giant bird on his back, I figured the Pontiac Firebird outside obviously belonged to him. Even though he was only 14 years older than I was, in many ways Don reminded me of my dad. They were both on the short side, with huge personalities. Big appetites, easy smiles, and bright eyes. Dad's were a warm brown, Don's were crystal blue. Much like my dad, if Don thought you were taking yourself too seriously, he would knock you down a notch.

Don's sense of humor always played against type. I saw people who thought they had a sense of who he was, with his commanding voice and his serious work ethic, then he would say something completely unexpected. He loved goofing on people to watch their reaction, especially his friends. Like the time Ann and I were hosting the AFTRA holiday party at our home in Beverly Hills.

Towards the end of the night, Don came up to Ann and me in the kitchen, our kids were standing there, too. Dayna was probably about 16 and Alex was 13. Don looked at the kids and said in an epic movie trailer voice, "Mommy's going to go away for a while and it's just going to be Uncle Don and your daddy living with you." Then he reached over and gave me a big kiss right on the lips. Ann and I about fell on the floor laughing along with our kids, but Don wasn't quite finished. With his hand planted on his hip, he said, "But we're not gonna live in this hellhole! We're all moving to MY house!"

Then there was the time Don overheard someone refer to me as the "Voice of FOX" broadcasting network. That was when I was voicing all of the network's comedies and Don was voicing

the dramas. He said, "Voice of FOX? That's who you are? Well, I bow to you Lord VOFF."

"Lord VOFF?"

"Yes indeed," he said. "You are Lord, Voice Of FOX, VOFF." He would needle me for the next few years, calling me Lord VOFF, but it never bothered me. In fact, I appreciated his friendly reminder to keep my feet planted firmly on the ground. Like my dad, Don didn't take any attitude from anybody, especially at work.

My guess is, if Don was tough on a producer, it was probably well deserved because Don knew just about everything there was to know about the business. He started out as a recording engineer, became a writer, producer, director, and eventually ended up doing voice-overs for the very commercials he used to create. Don had a huge vocabulary, he devoured books. He was one of the smartest guys I ever met. Don was the one who came up with that famous movie trailer line, the one that became the title of the movie, "In a world…" Every studio still used that line, long after he was gone. Don was famous for getting his reads right the first time around, so when a new producer tried to "direct" him, we all just sat back and waited for the sparks to fly. Not that he couldn't take direction, but let's face it, if someone's going to tell you what to do, they better know what they're talking about. It might go something like this:

"Very good, Mister LaFontaine. Now would you give me a second take on that?"

"Why?" It's only a three-letter word, but Don emphasized every letter, making it a complete sentence.

"Uh, so I have a backup take?"

"Why do you need another take of me doing what I just did?"

"Uh, you're right. Never mind, Mister LaFontaine."

Another time I heard a young producer say, "Let's do a 'tonight' version now."

Don replied, leaning into the microphone and in his very deepest register, "Normally I decide when that happens." The producer just froze, not knowing if Don was serious or not.

When he wasn't keeping me, and everyone else in check, Don enjoyed helping out newcomers who were trying hard to break into the voice-over business. I think it started when he was tooling around town in his limousine. Don and his driver would meet the lucky person at Don's agent's office, then take them on the ride of their life, going from session to session, watching and listening to everything he did. Don was so absolutely at the top of his game, it was a chance for the up-and-coming actor to learn at the foot of the master. I don't know how many people he invited to spend the day with him but I'm sure it was in the hundreds. It was incredibly generous. After Don passed away, his generosity was the inspiration behind building the Don LaFontaine Voice-Over Lab at the Screen Actors Guild Foundation in Los Angeles. Don's best friend, Paul Pape, and I came up with the idea to build a state-of-the-art recording studio that would be open, free of charge, to anyone who was interested in learning about the voice-over world. It's a place to experiment, make mistakes, and learn the craft without pressure or criticism. Paul and I call it a "virtual" ride-along with Don.

I never went on one of those ride-alongs. I was already working in voice-overs when he started his one-on-one sessions, but he did offer me advice at a time in my life when I thought my whole world was falling apart.

We were still living in Beverly Hills, when I found out I had been dropped by a very big client. With one phone call, I learned I had lost half of my income. I was sitting in my studio, paralyzed, feeling like I had just been punched in the stomach. It was devastating, the worst dive I had ever experienced on that terrible roller coaster. For the first time in my life I started to doubt myself. I thought my career was over.

Unfortunately, I had already committed to take part in a seminar that same week, in New York, promoting a book called "Secrets of Voice-Over Success." The book was the brainchild of actor, writer, and coach Joan Baker. It's filled with tips from some of the most successful voice-over actors around on how to get started in the business. The seminar was another chance to share those stories from some of us who wrote chapters in the book. Plus, all the proceeds from the sale of the book went towards Alzheimer's research, something I care about deeply. My own dad suffered from Alzheimer's disease. I knew there was no backing out from that trip. But all I could think of was, how could I take part in a discussion about voice-over success, when I felt like such a failure?

With a heavy heart I left my family back home in L.A. and flew to New York City. I knew that everyone on the voice-over panel would have heard about my personal disaster but I had no idea how they would treat me. After I landed at JFK Airport, I saw that I had a missed call on my cell phone from Don. He had left a message, inviting me up to his hotel room before the seminar that night. When I got there, he met me at the door of his beautiful suite at the Michelangelo Hotel, then grabbed me with both arms in a big hug. We sat down and right away he said to me, "Joey, don't worry about this. You're too good to not work."

Then he simply said, "Find your voice."

He went on to point out that the voice in which I was speaking to him at that moment was vastly different from the high-energy comedy performance I was known for at FOX, CBS, and other networks and shows. He told me to explore that voice. I didn't share his enthusiasm. In fact, I told him it had crossed my mind that my ride might be over, styles change, and all that. But he kept at it, encouraging me, propping me up, offering me comfort when I needed it most, from someone I greatly respected. I will always be grateful to him for his kindness and his compassion. Don gave me the confidence to carry on.

When I got back home, I did exactly what Don told me to do. I heard that NBC was looking for a new drama voice. I had never been hired to voice dramas before. I had never tapped into that lower register in my voice because I relied on the tried and true comedy sound. Now I had nothing to lose, so I went about creating a new voice-over demo, using my lower register for a series of drama promos. When I was done, I played it for my friends and agents. Not one person guessed it was me. But it was me, truly me, just a different version. A new attitude, a new voice. My agent Rita submitted my demo to NBC and I ended up getting the gig over scores of hopefuls. I met a whole new group of people in this new genre of voice-over, plus all kinds of unexpected opportunities suddenly opened up for me. Oddly enough, a few years later, the job I had originally lost, that caused so much worry in my life, ultimately came back to me.

Soon after I started working for NBC, I saw Don at a party where he was retelling this story from his perspective, meeting me in his hotel suite, hearing about the sudden loss of half my income, encouraging me to find my voice. When he finished the story, he leaned over to me and said, "Joey, you're a bigger man than me. If that had happened to me, I think I might have rolled up into the fetal position and not come out."

Of course, I don't think the great Don LaFontaine would have done that at all. He would have come out fighting, doing at least what I did, probably more. One thing I do know for sure. Don's concern and his words of encouragement, at possibly the lowest point in my voice-over career, helped me so much more than I can ever say.

In the 25 years I knew Don, I saw his image change from tacky to tasteful, his toupee tossed out in favor of shaving his head smooth, the flashy car traded in first for that limo, then for a more classic car. In my opinion, much of the credit for his sophisticated makeover goes to the wise and elegant Anita Whitaker LaFontaine, Don's talented wife. Together, Nita and Don loomed large in our small world of voice-over as a couple who cared deeply about sharing their success with others, whether they were opening their home to the rest of us for business meetings, or quietly donating to their favorite charities.

One year after Don died, an award was created at the worldwide television marketing convention, ProMax, in honor of his charitable acts. Nita graciously accepted on his behalf. The following year I was blown away to be the first to receive the award, following Don. That beautiful statue sits in my living room where I see it every day. It reminds me not to give up, to have faith in myself. Most of all it reminds me of Don's place in my life. I miss him. His jokes, his talent, his generous heart. I will never forget how Don inspired me to find all of my voices, especially at that time when I felt so lost.

As much as Don helped me with my career, there was another voice-over actor who made a huge impression on my personal life. His name was Danny Dark. You may remember I was inspired to use the name Dave Donovan early in my radio career by a few great "Double D's." Danny was one of them, at the top of the heap. We all called Danny Dark, D Squared. When I was coming

up in radio, Danny was the voice of everything. I absolutely idolized him. "This Bud's for you." "Anheuser-Busch, St. Louis." "Raid! Kills-Bugs-Dead." Keebler cookies, "baked by little elves in a hollow tree." StarKist tuna, "Sorry, Charlie." And so many more iconic advertising lines. Danny was also one of the last great network voices, working for NBC for more than 15 years. That was back in the day when one person voiced all shows the network had on the air, dramas, comedies, live shows, and movies. He was a king among princes.

When Danny opened his mouth, it sounded like honey oozing out of a fluffy white cloud. Like warm butter spread out on a slice of homemade bread just out of the oven. His cadence was cool, his voice was hip, and his rhythm was pure jazz. I think he visited us from a time gone by, a different era. Every time I saw him I felt as if I had traveled back to the days of F. Scott Fitzgerald and "The Great Gatsby." It was like being best friends with Errol Flynn, as much for the mischief Danny caused as for the natural suave, debonair, smooth way about him. Danny would wear an ascot and carry it off without a hitch. He charmed everyone he met, immediately holding them in the palm of his hand just by the easy, dreamy way he said "hello."

For all of his polish, Danny was also a real man's man. He lived life to the fullest. He was about my height, but when he grabbed you for a hug it felt like he was ten feet tall. He called everybody honey or baby and it never sounded strange. The moment he met you he would give you a nickname. Mine was Josie. Josie honey, Josie baby, Josie boy, or any other combination that sounded good to him.

I first met Danny in 1989 at his movie-star home in Brentwood, off Sunset Boulevard. Danny and his wife, JoBee, had opened up their home for a meeting of AFTRA, our voice-over union. Here was another legendary guy, inviting us rank-and-file members into his living room, to rub elbows with the big guns.

But it wasn't until my agent Rita asked me to meet with Danny that I actually worked up the confidence to talk to him.

It was in the spring of 1994, right about the time home studios were becoming more common for voice-over actors. Because of my technical background, skills I had learned from my dad, I was one of the first guys to build my own studio at home, setting up an ISDN line and dialing in to the FOX network for my sessions at night. Rita wanted me to show Danny the ropes so he could build his own studio, too. I told Rita to ask Danny if he'd be willing to come over for one of my afternoon sessions – and he was. I set up an extra chair next to the audio board, along with a microphone and headphones, so he could listen to both sides of the conversation.

A date was made and a week after Rita's call, the doorbell rang about 30 minutes before the network was supposed to dial me up, plenty of time for us to get acquainted. I opened the door to greet the very dapper, the very charming Danny Dark. He was holding a brown paper bag filled with ripe tomatoes just picked from his garden at home.

"Hi Josie. Here's a gift for you and Annie. Thanks for the help," he said. I doubt that Danny ever showed up to someone's house empty-handed.

We went downstairs to my studio where he slipped on those headphones and let loose with a little love into his microphone. When we hooked up with the studio at FOX, he knew everyone in the room, the mixer, the producer, they all joked and chatted about their past encounters. Working this way was a whole new experience for Danny. He thought the idea of having a studio at home was pure genius, saving him the ride from the west side of Los Angeles, all the way to NBC in Burbank. He was interested in learning everything there was to know about building a studio.

We hit it off right away, and talked until it was nearly dark. As he got up to leave, I somewhat offhandedly said we should get together for dinner sometime, with our wives. Danny said, "Sure, when?" I probably said something like, "I'm not sure. Let's figure it out later," but he wouldn't let it go. He said, "Get out your calendar and let's pick a date right now." Danny was like that. He never left things ambiguous. If you said we should have dinner sometime, he said, "When?" That's one of the many wonderful gifts I picked up from D Squared.

Our first double date was at Peppone's restaurant, an old-style, red-sauce Italian restaurant, just down the street from his house. Ann and I fell in love with Danny's wife, JoBee, and the four of us became fast friends. JoBee is the most warm, beautiful, absolutely fun person you could ever want to know, extremely talented in so many ways, first and foremost as a dancer and choreographer, and also a gifted photographer. Together they were the cutest couple ever. Love birds. One night we were having dinner at the Hotel Bel-Air, kind of a quiet, stuffy old restaurant, when he looked over at me and hollered out across the table, "Our wives are so freakin' HOTTTT!" All heads turned in our direction as I looked back at Danny admitting, that yes, he spoke the truth.

Those dinners were the beginning of many years of adventures with Danny. I remember one time when Ann and I were spending the weekend in Malibu with our kids. Danny called to chat, I told him where we were and he said, "Hang on honey, I'm comin' over. I got us a couple of Cubanos that need to be fired up."

"Okay Double D, I'll be here."

Danny and JoBee had just been on a trip to France and he had brought back two beautiful Cuban cigars. We sat out on the beach, lit up those cigars, and caught up on his escapades in the City of Light. After a while I asked him to take me on a tour of

his Malibu days. Danny used to own a big home on Malibu Road and I had always wondered where it was, so off we went. I tossed Danny the keys to my convertible and said, "You drive," and we hit the road. He showed me his old house and a few other of his favorite haunts, then said, "You've gotta check this out," and he pulled up to the entrance of Serra Retreat, a gated, private community in the heart of Malibu. I wondered how we were going to get in, but I forgot whom I was with for a moment. We pulled up to the guard gate, the security man stepped out with a skeptical look and coolly said, "Can I help you?" Danny looked over with a big smile on his face, a curl of smoke streaming from the cigar hanging out of his mouth, "Hey, honey, how are you today? Listen, man, I'm Danny Dark and this is my buddy Josie Cipriano. We'd like to head in to your fancy place here just to take a look around." For whatever reason the security guard answered, "Of course, Mister Dark. Drive carefully."

What? Danny was just so cool, outrageously hip, so purely honest and transparent, the guard was disarmed. We went on our tour, as Danny pointed out where all the celebrities lived, then after we'd seen it all, he turned the car around, waving to the guard as we drove out of the gate. The longer I knew him, the more I realized Danny probably got away with everything he ever wanted to do in his life. His daughter once told me that when she was a kid, Danny would barge into her room late at night, wake her up at three in the morning to say, "Honey, let's have a candy party!" and they would, right there in the middle of the night.

The craziest stories I remember about Danny happened in New York. The first time was in December, just after Christmas. Ann and I were there with our kids, visiting my family. Danny and JoBee were in the city, celebrating their anniversary. The four of us had dinner at Cipriani's on Fifth Avenue, then headed out of the restaurant to continue our celebration. We decided to walk

from Cipriani's to the Monkey Bar on 54th Street, eager to enjoy the last of the holiday decorations. It was a bitter, cold night. We were bundled up in long coats with scarves wrapped around our necks. Danny and I warmed up with a couple of cigars, while JoBee snapped a few pictures. When we got to the bar, it was like stepping back in time, not an unfamiliar feeling when you're with Danny.

The Monkey Bar was dark, warm, with a couple of guys playing jazz and a few late-night couples swaying to the music on the dance floor. Annie, JoBee, Danny, and I took four seats at the bar. By then we had finished our cigars, and we ordered a few drinks. This was so long ago, you could still smoke inside a restaurant, so Danny took out his pipe, already stuffed with weed, and lit up. Danny always had his pipe at the ready. It just so happened he was ready at that moment. We chatted with the bartender, sipped our drinks, and swapped stories. Suddenly, as the bartender was cleaning glasses with his back to us, he caught a whiff of something he hadn't expected. I saw him stiffen, he turned to look over his shoulder and cocked his head, trying to figure out where the marijuana smell was coming from, but nothing made sense. His gaze landed on the dapper gentleman with the scarf draped around his neck and the natty clothes, with a pipe stuck between his teeth. The bartender tipped his head to one side, narrowed one eye then shook his head as if to say, "Couldn't be."

Yeah, it could. And it would, over and over. Ann and I were in New York again staying at Trump International at Columbus Circle and Danny and JoBee were in the city too, staying at the St. Regis Hotel. It was a crisp, rainy fall day this time when I called Danny to say, "Hey D Squared, wanna go to the Grand Havana Room for an after-dinner drink and cigars?" He said, "Hell, yeah." I grabbed a cab and told Danny I would swing by

his place to pick him up. Pulling up to that legendary St. Regis canopy on 58th Street as I looked out through the raindrops staining the window of my taxi, I saw a man wearing an elegant long coat with a cool fedora covering his head. The doorman held a huge umbrella above him for protection from the cold rain as Mr. Danny Dark stepped off the curb and into the cab. With Danny in place we were off for 666 Avenue of the Americas, once known as "Top of The Sixes." Our destination was the penthouse and the private cigar club, The Grand Havana Room. Since I was a member of the original in Beverly Hills, I had residual membership at the New York club, too.

We found ourselves a couple of chairs in the corner of the club, looking up Avenue of the Americas through floor-to-ceiling corner windows, watching the rainfall outside. I had a cigar and Danny lit up his corncob pipe. Sitting next to us was a big group having a great time. At some point we realized that one of the people in the group was the remarkable actor and dancer, the late Gregory Hines. He had a show on CBS at the time called, what else but "The Gregory Hines Show," and I was voicing the promos for the show. Danny got up to introduce himself to Gregory, then brought me up and said, "Gregory, Josie here is the voice of your show on CBS." Gregory said, "What? You're kidding. Let me hear." I did a promo for his show and he fell down laughing. He introduced us to all of his friends and we chatted for quite a while before heading back to our chairs. It was another great night, talking, smoking, me with my cigar, Danny with a pipe full of weed. It had gotten to be about two in the morning and we were just about the last people in the club when I said, "Danny, we should be getting back to our wives." He agreed.

As we left the club, headed to the elevators, Danny stopped to have a chat with the manager, to thank him for a wonderful night. Danny walked off to the elevators, as I shook the manager's hand

and thanked him, too. He gently grabbed my arm and drew me close and said in confidence, "It was a pleasure, Mr. Cipriano, but may I make a suggestion?"

I said, "Of course."

He said, "The next time Mr. Dark joins us, could you please encourage him to enjoy one of our fine cigars instead of his pipe?"

I said, "Good call. Yes, I'll be sure to do that."

I had many memorable times together with Danny but sadly, a short ten years after the start of our great friendship, he became gravely ill and his sickness happened way too fast. It was in 2004 when I saw him for the last time. The four of us went out to dinner, at the Hotel Bel-Air once again. JoBee had warned me ahead of time that Danny was in a lot of pain, but when we got there, I couldn't see any signs of the discomfort or struggle he was feeling. Somehow, Danny was the same man I knew so well, charming the maître d', the waiter, the busboy, everyone. He was dressed to the nines in a perfectly tailored sports jacket with a tie. JoBee was beautiful as well, hiding any of the sadness that I knew she was feeling inside. Instead I saw the love and happiness of Danny enjoying himself, one more time.

We had a wonderful time and he and I talked often on the phone after that night, but several weeks later, Danny was gone. I was honored when his family asked me to be the emcee at Danny's memorial tribute at the Sportsman's Lodge in Studio City. Walking through the door is like stepping back in time to the fifties, the perfect setting for Danny. It was a tough day but also a celebration of his life with so many wonderful stories about this special man. A beautiful way to say goodbye to one of my best friends.

As for JoBee, our friendship continues stronger than ever.

During the Danny and JoBee years, I first meet JoBee's beautiful daughter Janeen and her husband, Michael Damian. Today, I consider Michael one of my closest friends and the five of us never go more than a few weeks without seeing one another, continuing the tradition of great meals and fun adventures. If it weren't for Danny, I wouldn't have these beautiful people in my life today.

A couple of months after Danny's death, I was talking to JoBee on the phone, and we were about to hang up when I could tell she had something else to say. She hesitated, then told me she needed to ask a favor. I said, "Of course, anything."

She said, "Danny made me promise something to him during those last weeks of his life. And Joe, I know you are the only person who can help me with this."

I couldn't imagine. I braced myself and then she told me. "Danny worked at a lot of studios, a lot of networks, but there was one he was especially fond of. Danny said, 'Honey, when I'm gone, I want you to spread my ashes all over that fucking place.'"

That's not at all what I expected her to say. I didn't know whether to laugh or cry and as I rolled this around in my head, I had no idea how we were going to get the job done. I told Ann about it and asked her to help. A few weeks had gone by and we were supposed to meet up with JoBee on a Wednesday afternoon, but we still didn't have a solid plan. Earlier that day Ann was having lunch with some of her closest friends at an outdoor café. She was with Deborah Lloyd, our good friend Suzy Stromsborg, and her sister Christy Farmer when Ann told them what was going on. Christy came up with an offbeat suggestion, one that was actually staring them right in the face. Why not grab a couple of those take-out coffee cups and lids from the counter right next to them, and use those to carry out Danny's wishes? We could pour his ashes into the cups, then sprinkle him around without

tipping off anyone. It was the only idea we had, so that's exactly what we did.

Ann picked up JoBee at her house and the two of them drove together to meet up with me. This was the exact time of my life when I was working all over town, at several studios, production companies, and networks where Danny used to work. It was Don LaFontaine's advice that gave me the courage to go after new jobs. But I always thought Danny had something to do with landing them. I chalked it up to some sort of supernatural intervention from D Squared. Now that JoBee had dropped this bomb on me, I knew it must be true. There wasn't any other way we would have been able to get into some of those places, unless I worked there, too.

We met up at a park, near one of the networks. I had no doubt Danny probably spent some time smoking his precious pipe, sitting at one of the picnic tables under a tree in that park. JoBee pulled out the wood box with Danny's remains and we stared at it for a moment. I don't think any of us wanted to make the first move. JoBee opened it up and I carefully began to pour Danny's ashes into our coffee cups. We needed a little practice, so we started by leaving a little bit of Danny here and there outside in the park. Once that was done, we headed over to the studio.

We walked in through the gate where we chatted with the guard, carefully setting our official Danny Dark "coffee cups" on the counter top. There was no turning back now. The guard let us pass and wished us well. As we walked through the door we began to spread Danny everywhere. Some of him ended in his old parking space, some of Danny went into the engineering area, some in one of the sound stages. But my favorite spot was in the stairwell, on the way to the audio rooms. That's where Danny came in and out of his recording sessions so many days of his life. That's where I went to work now, too, up and down those exact same stairs. Everywhere Danny went, that's where we took him on his last visit.

We had one moment of panic, when we thought we were being followed. Ann saw a security guard walking behind us, and when we turned the corner, he turned the corner. We went through a door, he went through the door. Ann broke out in a sweat and JoBee was as pale as the cup in her hand. I was about to lose it when we turned right and he turned left. We were safe to finish the job but after that scare we left in a hurry.

For the rest of my time at that network, whenever I took those stairs to the audio rooms, I would tip my imaginary hat to Danny and say, "Hey Danny, how ya doin'?" On my way out, at the end of the day, I'd say, "See you tomorrow, D-Squared."

Danny was a legend, and he got a legendary send-off. We spread his ashes all over that fucking place.

Back when I first met Danny and we became close, it was at a turning point in his life. Danny's reign as one of the most accomplished voice-over talents in television was just about to come to an end. He had been one of the most recognizable voices on network TV when gradually, the calls stopped coming. It wasn't just the drop in income that saddened him, it was the loss of his identity as a network talent as well. The calls for commercials stopped coming too. It's inevitable; it's the nature of most every business. You're up, then you're down. Hopefully, you find your way back up again.

I caught Danny at a time when he was healing from the slipping away of his career. Yet even though he felt abandoned, he still had great laughter and love in his personal life. He pushed past the sadness to embrace the joy. Danny and JoBee traveled the world, he took up piano lessons, played his trumpet, did whatever he wanted to do, whenever he had the thought. That's the gift he gave me. His most important piece of advice. No matter what is going on in your life, you should always make time for a candy party.

On the air at KIIS AM, 1987. How the mediocre have fallen.

KIIS FM's Big Ron O'Brien and Tim Kelly at my house for a 4th of July party.

My dad in the studio we built in our Pacific Palisades house.

My big brother Hank and me with my mom and dad at their 50th Wedding Anniversary party.

Surrounded by brilliance with Ron Scalera on the left and Geoff Calnan on the right.

Ann and me at one of the huge FOX Image Campaign shoots in 1989.

Getting a "buss" from the great Don LaFontaine, 1999.

Cipriani's in New York with the legendary Danny Dark and his beautiful wife, JoBee.

Danny had his pipe somewhere on him as we walked on 5th Avenue to the Monkey Bar in New York.

The Loop Group.

With John Lloyd and Tony Bennett at Royal Albert Hall, London.

The Primetime Voices Photo Shoot.

We all chipped in to buy this ad congratulating Don LaFontaine on his Lifetime
Achievement Award.

La famiglia Cipriano.

Sushi Night at the Cips with Michelle Robie, Ron Scalera, Ann, Elizabeth Scalera and Paul Robie.

Gone way too soon and way too sad.

Construction of the Don LaFontaine Voice Over Lab, with studio designer, George Whittam.

With co-founders, George Whittam and Paul Pape at the completed DLFVO Lab.

168

Celebrating with Ann after I received the DLF Legacy Award.

Proof that you don't always get all the gigs, but it was fun trying out for it.
With Vanna White and Pat Sajak.

170

When Chef Morimoto speaks on Iron Chef America, my voice comes out.

Another Loop Group Makimoto Monday.

The Primetime Voices for Children visit the Mattel Children's Hospital, UCLA.

On set for "In a World..." with Alexandra Holden, Fred Melamed, Ken Marino, Marc Graue, and Mark Elliot. That's writer, director, and star Lake Bell in the middle.

With Lake Bell at The Sundance Film Festival 2013 where she won the Waldo Salt Screenwriters Award for "In a World..."

Hangin' in the Clubhouse.

My home studio.

LADIES AND GENTLEMEN, PLEASE WELCOME...

The first time I ever announced a live television show, I nearly blew it. It was 1996 and I just got hired to work on the VH1 Honors, broadcasting live from the Universal Amphitheater, in Los Angeles. When I walked in for rehearsal, I guess I expected the booth to be someplace special, right next to the stage, in a trailer, or even at the back of the theater. But that's not where I ended up. I was UNDER the stage, in the basement of the amphitheater. The stage manager led me down a set of dark, dreary, cement stairs into the bowels of the building. Welcome to show business, I thought.

At the bottom of the steps we entered a vast room that looked like a warehouse. We walked past electrical panels and I could see ductwork snaking around everywhere. Planted smack in the middle of all that emptiness was a bunch of scaffolding, holding up thick drapes to create a makeshift booth. Inside my little room was a folding table, with a small television set, headphones, a microphone, and a box with a couple of buttons on it. This was not the glamorous setup I had expected for something called the VH1 Honors.

Just then the rehearsal started upstairs, with the unmistakable thumping of a rock band performing on stage, right above our heads. Huge equipment was moved onto and then off of the stage. It was loud! The equipment rumbled above me and the percussive beat of the rock bands shook the ceiling and rattled my little table. The only other time I had a similar shaking experience was live on the air at KIIS-FM when an earthquake hit at the exact same time I was playing the song "Causing a Commotion" by Madonna.

The stage manager showed me how the control box worked. That's what I would use to communicate with the director of the show, a nice guy named Dan Appel. One button turned the microphone on and off and the other one would allow me to talk to Dan. If I had a question, all I had to do was push the button to reach him in the truck outside where the crew was set up. There were also two volume-control knobs, one for the programming audio in my ear, and one to control the volume of the director's talkback and all the other myriad of sounds coming from the truck, from the camera people, lighting people, and stage managers. I learned quickly there is a lot of chatter and surprisingly a lot of yelling going on in your ear all during a live show.

Once the show started, everything was going smoothly. For me there's nothing better than following along in my own fat, three-ring binder, stuffed with the script of a live show, and being a page or two away from a live-announce moment. It's exciting, it's fast-paced, and everyone is pumped. I heard the director say, "Item 46 is next. Joe, that's you. We have a live announce coming out of the band and introducing Cameron Diaz." I clicked my talkback mic and said, "Got it."

As the band finished its number, applause broke out in the house, when I heard in my headphones from the director, "Ready announce...annnnd cue announce." That's my cue. I tapped the button for the microphone. The button lit up, and opened my mic into the auditorium, live on the air. Loud and proud I said, "Ladies and gentlemen, please welcome the..."

Suddenly I heard director Dan Appel say, "No, no, no, no... stop...stop." I froze. I stopped talking. Then I heard Dan say, "Joe, what are you doing? Why the fuck did you stop talking??? GO GO GO GO."

I immediately picked up where I left off and introduced Cameron Diaz.

That's when I learned a very important lesson about live announcing. All those other voices in your ear, the camera folks, lighting, stage manager, who the hell knows who else, the director communicates with all of them, and they are all on the same talkback channel that he uses for the announcer. Me. On my first live-announce gig. When he said, "No, no, no, no...stop, stop," he wasn't talking to me, he was shouting at a cameraman who was moving in the wrong direction.

From that moment on, I decided if I ever announced another live show, when the director says, "ready announce...cue announce," I would turn DOWN the volume of the truck, start reading the script, and just keep going. My thinking was, if the director says CUE ANNOUNCE...I'm gonna go announce and nothing will ever stop me again. Ever. If they made a mistake in cuing me, too bad. I'm taking the ball down the field and I'm scoring a touchdown even if I'm running the wrong way.

After that show I did get plenty of other live announcing jobs. I was the hot sound of the moment and the offers kept rolling in, "Vanessa Williams and Friends," "Elton John, Live," and the most fun of all, "The Blockbuster Entertainment Awards." My biggest supporter in the world of live TV shows was the brilliant producer/director Ken Ehrlich. My guess is that Ken has produced more shows, and the best shows, about music than anyone else, at any time, anywhere. I think he personally knows every rock star, past and present, and just about every actor, singer, and celebrity on the planet. He is incomparable, the coolest cat around at what he does. No one puts on a show like Ken.

The very first "Blockbuster Entertainment Awards" went on the air in 1997, from the Pantages Theater in Hollywood. To this day I still think it was the most exciting of all the awards shows because it included stars from movies, television, and music. There was every big name in the world appearing on that one stage. Best of all, my announce booth was not UNDER the stage, anymore. It was right smack-dab in the middle of all the action, backstage.

The way the Pantages Theater was set up, when you walked off stage, you went down a couple of steps, into an open area with a couple of hallways leading to about 25 or 30 dressing rooms. My booth was one of those dressing rooms, right in the center of everything and everyone, including John Travolta, Tom Cruise, Antonio Banderas, Ben Affleck, Drew Barrymore, Warren Beatty, Jim Carrey, Courteney Cox, Russell Crowe, Harrison Ford, Tom Green, Kate Hudson, Michelle Pfeiffer, Keanu Reeves, Ben Stiller, Clooney, Crystal, Costner, Cube (as in Ice), Jamie Lee Curtis, the list went on and on and on. It was like a night of a thousand stars, with all of those people crisscrossing from make-up room

to dressing room, from dressing room to the green room where the producers set up food and drinks, from the green room to the stage, this way and that way, everyone stopped to chat with one another. I felt like I was hanging out by my locker in between classes, if my high school happened to be Hollywood High.

With all of those people standing around, the last thing I wanted to do was shut myself off from the fun. I love to be in on the action, so what did I do? I left my dressing room door/ voice-over booth wide open. Everybody who walked off that stage could see me and hear me doing my live announcing thing. They'd poke their head in and say, "You're kidding! You're live on the air from right HERE?" I got to meet everyone. It was a blast. Tom Hanks called out to Harrison Ford, "Do you see this guy? He's got the best gig ever. Joe, how can I get into this line of work?" I told him I thought his career was going just fine. The other cool thing for me was, the show didn't have a host, so as the announcer, I introduced absolutely everything that happened on stage.

As the show got into its second and third year, Ken let me bring my family, Ann, Dayna, and Alex, and a bunch of other people, too. One year my brother Henry and sister-in-law Eileen came out from Connecticut to go to the show with our friends Peter and Patti Black. We hired a limo to take us back and forth and on the way home, in true Hollywood style, stopped off at In 'N Out Burger for dinner to cap off the night.

If you're lucky enough to be asked back to voice the same live show, sometimes the producer will throw in a couple of extra perks. Especially if the salary stays the same, at least you can up the ante with some fringe benefits. After the first few years, I

was able to get all-access passes for Dayna and Alex. If you think I was having fun backstage, my kids had the run of the house, and brought their friends with them, too. Dayna sat in the front row when 'N Sync rehearsed a number for one of the shows, then ran backstage during the live broadcast for a picture with Justin Timberlake. Alex had his best friend Christopher Moore with him one year when the cast of "Charlie's Angels" walked off stage. The boys got a photo with Drew Barrymore, Lucy Liu, and Cameron Diaz crouching down to be at the same height as the two 12-year-olds. Cameron Diaz had her arm draped around Alex with her head on his shoulder. Golden.

The most fun I ever had working would probably be those Blockbuster Entertainment shows. It was a party. Loose, loud, and lively. The audience was encouraged to scream and shout out to the stars. When the actors and singers walked onto the stage, they were greeted with deafening roars from the crowd. They would look out in amazement at that beautiful theater, all the way up to the elaborate gold balconies high above the stage. I could actually see them on camera mouth the word "WOW."

I had several great years working that show when it all came to an end in 2001. That's when Blockbuster pulled the plug on its live television show. I think security concerns after 9/11 made it a tough show to produce. Also, the Blockbuster company was probably just beginning its downward slide about that time. New technology had already started to take over the movie rental business, like satellite TV and Netflix. Boy, do I miss those shows. But I wasn't done yet. Turned out I was just getting started in the live-announce business.

It was February 2000 when Ken hired me to say the following

words, "Live from Los Angeles, welcome to music's biggest night!" That was my very first Grammy Awards show. Talk about the big time, that show is seen around the world in I don't know how many countries. Even today, just thinking about it puts a smile on my face. The host that year was Rosie O'Donnell. I was back for two more years after that when Jon Stewart hosted both of those shows. During that time the Grammys were broadcast from three different theaters, first the Dorothy Chandler Pavilion, then Staples Center, and finally the new Nokia Theater. For all three of those shows the announce booth was in the audience, in a small room at the back of the theater.

Working on the Grammys was such a rush of adrenaline. I still left my door open, something I learned doing the Blockbuster shows. During the telecast when I didn't have anything to say, I wandered out into the aisle to talk to people in the audience. No more running backstage, though. Times had changed. I don't think I had ever before seen such tight security at a television show. It was a privilege to be part of a combined effort of hundreds of professionals working together for weeks and weeks of planning, for that one moment to pull it all off, LIVE. Thank you, Ken. Working for you is an honor, my own lifetime achievement award.

All the time I was announcing those live shows, I was still doing promos, as well. Remember when I was first hired at FOX? Bob and Lew picked me to voice the promos for the Primetime Emmy Awards. That was back in 1988. Seventeen years later, I was the live announcer for the actual Emmy broadcast. That didn't take too long, did it? The first year, 2005, Ellen DeGeneres was the host, at the Shrine Auditorium in downtown L.A., then I

did the show when five reality stars hosted, followed by my most recent Emmy gig, with Conan O'Brien. Conan was just gearing up for his move from New York to Los Angeles to take over the "Tonight Show" from Jay Leno. We all know how that ended up. But at the time we were doing the Emmys, that move was still in the future for Conan and I had a lot of fun chatting with him during rehearsals about what his life would be like in L.A. I mentioned to him that he didn't meet the height restriction for late-night hosts in Los Angeles, citing the many low bridges and tree-covered streets around town. He told me not to worry, that NBC had ordered he be shortened upon crossing the state line.

On most of the bigger live shows, like the Grammys and the Emmys, the announcer has his or her own script assistant by their side, in the booth. That's a big help when it comes to pronouncing some of the names of the winners. I couldn't exactly turn off the microphone, or the transmitter, like I did when I worked at WWCO in Connecticut, just because I wasn't sure how to pronounce the winner of best polka album.

Walking the red carpet at those events was an unexpected thrill, especially at the Emmys. There are actually two carpets at most award shows. One is for the nominees and big-name stars, and the other one is for ticket holders, us common people. Of course I snuck onto the major one as often as possible, walking the carpet at least two or three times at each event. Ann's sister Amy went with us to the show when Ellen DeGeneres hosted, along with our friends Patti and Deb Lloyd. Come to think of it, Patti has been to quite a few of my live-announcing jobs. They walked the carpet, too. We taped the pre-show back home and there they were, in the background, watching all the celebrities

getting interviewed. They looked beautiful.

Working on live shows, like most other voice-over work, was mainly a male-dominated industry until just a few years go. I give a lot of credit to Randy Thomas, one of the best female voices in the business, for crashing through that glass ceiling. Randy has announced the Oscars, Emmys, and Tonys. Because of her success, and a change in thinking by producers, just about every live show on television these days has a female announcer. Voice-over artists like Melissa Disney, Ellen K, and Cedering Fox have taken over all of the big live events. Even if that means less work for me, I am happy to see the transformation. It's about time.

One of the most famous live-show announcers ever is the incomparable Don Pardo. Most people my age remember him from game shows but my own kids know him from "Saturday Night Live," where he is still part of that iconic introduction, "Liiiiiive from New Yoirk, it's Saturday Night Looooiiiiive!" I actually met Don a long time ago when I was 19 years old. It happened in New York City, when a friend of mine from WWCO radio got tickets to see the taping of a game show called "Winning Streak." My buddy, Fred Landau, was a sports reporter at C-O and he was auditioning to be a contestant. When I heard that Don Pardo was the announcer for "Winning Streak," I knew I had to see it first-hand. I was more interested in working ON a show, rather than being a contestant IN a show. Fred was from New Jersey and had been to New York plenty of times. I had only been to Manhattan one other time in my entire life. I was happy to let Fred lead the way.

"Winning Streak" was taped at NBC Rockefeller Center, in the heart of the city. Fred got us there early enough to get good

seats for the taping. When they let us into the studio, I walked straight down to the first row, right in front of the podium where the microphone was set up. Ten minutes before the show was supposed to start, out walked Don Pardo. Immediately, I could see in his eyes just how much he loved his job. I wanted that exact same feeling. He faced an audience filled with happy people, all wide-eyed, and excited to hear what he had to say.

First off Don said hello and welcomed everyone to the show. Then he went through a quick rundown of how a taping worked. He pointed out the applause signs above our heads and ran through a couple of rehearsals. Every time the applause sign blinked, he urged us to clap and yell louder and louder. Each time he called out, "I can't hear YOOOO!" encouraging us to make more noise. All around us the studio came alive. Cameramen took their positions, other men pulled cables across the stage, checked the lighting, someone else sorted out index cards for the host of the show, Bill Cullen. Game sounds were tested, buzzers and bells, the game board flashed on and off, there was nonstop action as the director got ready to count down to the open of the show. While all this went on, Don Pardo continued to talk to the audience in a friendly, casual manner. He sipped on his coffee, made jokes with the script people and producers, and confided in all of us in the audience little inside stories about the show.

"One minute to go," the stage manager called out. I looked over at a huge clock on the wall that ticked down to when the show would begin. Most game shows are taped as if they were live broadcasts. It helps the pace of the show and keeps the audience involved. As the clock ticked down to 45 seconds, Don looked at me, sitting right in front of him, and noticed I was craning my

neck, trying to get a look at his script.

Speaking into his microphone so the audience could hear, he said, "Hey, what's your name, kid?"

"Uh, Dave Cipriano."

"Thirty seconds to go," yelled the stage manager.

"Cipriano huh? D'you run that restaurant Cipriani's on 5th Avenue?"

The audience laughed. Twenty seconds.

I said, "No, I missed out on being a millionaire by having an 'o' on the end of my name instead of an 'i.'"

"Ten seconds," from the stage manager.

Don turned to the audience and said, "Quick, kid. So what do you wanna do when you grow up, kid?"

"Five seconds!"

I had to answer honestly.

"Well, I'd really like to have your job, Mister Pardo." The audience laughed.

"Good luck with that, kid. I ain't givin' it up for a long while." The audience howled at that.

"Three, two, one." A moment of absolute silence.

The music started and Don winked at me as he turned to his microphone and bellowed out in that unmistakable voice that has since launched a thousand "Saturday Night Live" broadcasts...

"The stakes get higher as the words get longer in 'Winnnning Streak.' And now here's your host...Bill Cullen."

APPLAUSE – APPLAUSE the sign blinked madly. The crowd clapped, cheered, even whistled with excitement. People were up on their feet, smiling. For most of us it was the first time we had ever been to a game show. I might have been a seasoned deejay back home in Connecticut, but this was New York City. NBC. Rockefeller Plaza. Don Pardo. It was like taking a peek behind the curtain at the great Wizard of Oz. And I was hooked.

I'M GAME FOR GAME SHOWS

Ever since I saw Don Pardo charm a studio audience on "Winning Streak," I wanted to work on a game show. It was 1997 when I got a job on "Pictionary," based on the board game of the same name. You always remember your first and I have some indelible memories from doing over 110 episodes of that show.

"Pictionary" turned out to be just the beginning. After that, I was hired to be the announcer for "Deal or No Deal," "Amnesia," "Identity," "Superstars of Dance," "Thank God You're Here," and "One vs. 100" hosted by Bob Saget. I first met Bob when our kids went to grammar school together in Pacific Palisades. We were drop-off and pick-up dads for a number of years and participated in fund-raisers for the school. When I started on "One vs. 100," Bob was at the post studio for a couple of audio pickups as I walked in. "You're kidding me," he said. "You're the announcer!? This is great, it's like family."

"One vs. 100" had a pretty good run and Bob was a very funny host, but they were all eclipsed by "Deal or No Deal."

Working on "Deal" was high energy and pure fun. I got that job back in 2005 when I was doing the drama promos for NBC. Hosted by Howie Mandel, "Deal" had a limited run in December where it did very well. I was hired to do a couple of promos for the

show, when NBC decided to stay with it and put it on the regular primetime schedule. The executive producer, Scott St. John, had heard me on a couple of the promos and told his show runner to get that voice guy at the network to be the announcer on "Deal."

I did all my work in post-production, when they packaged the final product. Howie Mandel came to the post studio as well to pick up audio for some of his lines that needed to be recorded for audio problems or copy changes. Whenever I watched the show on TV, or saw Howie at the post studio, he looked like he was in heaven. The show was a huge hit, a cultural phenomenon, and it seemed to me that he loved every minute of it. In fact, I think everyone enjoyed being a part of the "Deal" experience, even the producers. They put on some extravagant holiday parties each year, as a big thank you to the cast and crew. I know I sure had a blast.

In December of 2007, I got a call from the production office saying, "Howie has a Christmas gift for you and we would like to come deliver it." I couldn't imagine what it was. About an hour later, our doorbell rang and there was a guy outside holding up a beautiful, shiny new bicycle. He wheeled it into our living room, flipped down the kickstand and off he went to the next delivery. It was a glossy black-and-yellow Beach Cruiser, decorated with logos all over it, Howie Mandel's face, the iconic NBC logo, and decals with "Deal or No Deal" plastered everywhere. Howie must have bought scores of those bikes and gave them out to everyone who worked on the show. I love mine and if you're ever at Santa Monica or Venice Beach on a warm Sunday morning and see a "Deal or No Deal" bike dashing by, take a closer look. That's me.

Even though I don't get to see Howie these days, I'm the announcer on another show he does called "America's Got Talent." My part for "AGT" was just the intro of the show and I actually recorded the whole season in one session. Most recently I was the announcer for "Hollywood Game Night," hosted by Jane

Lynch, on NBC. I look at each one of those shows as another adventure and always learn something new from the people I meet. But without a doubt, the most memorable game show of all was my very first one, "Pictionary."

The host was Alan Thicke. He played the dad on the TV sitcom "Growing Pains," and in real life he's the dad of singer Robin Thicke. We taped every other weekend, five shows on Saturday and five more on Sunday, at CBS Television City, in Hollywood, the same place I did promos for the CBS network. It was a thrill to finally have a shot at doing a game show. The studio where we taped was legendary Stage 33, the same one used for "The Price is Right," so that put a big check mark in the box I have for Hollywood tradition. I loved exploring backstage and talking to the crew, hearing stories of past glories in that studio.

Not only was I doing the announcing for "Pictionary," I was also hired to do the warm-up before the show. When I saw Don Pardo do it back at NBC in New York, it looked kind of easy, very natural. He came out to his microphone about five minutes before the show started, said a few funny lines to the audience, bantered with the staff, made a few more jokes and then introduced the beginning of the show. That's not how we did it at "Pictionary."

My daily routine went something like this. I arrived at CBS on Saturday and Sunday mornings at about nine o'clock. The first thing I did was head to the stage and pop my head into Alan Thicke's dressing room. I never knew what I was going to get on any given morning with Alan. Sometimes he was charming, other times if something wasn't going right, it seemed to me he'd be in a mood. One time I popped in and the makeup artist was working on him, she looked at me and rolled her eyes. I took that as a sign, something was up. Alan caught sight of me in his makeup mirror and I remember him asking how I was doing, in a kind of gloomy voice. "I'm great, Alan, everything's great," I

chirped back. I saw him narrow his gaze at my reflection in the mirror as he told me I obviously didn't know what the hell was going on because the fucking place was falling apart. I'd chuckle at his remarks. I found his idiosyncrasies entertaining and truth be told, he's known for a rather cynical, wry sense of humor. I never took any of it personally.

After that quick check-in I'd head up to my dressing room to prepare for the day's taping. At about ten thirty, my favorite part of the day, I went down to the set and walked onto that stage while the crew was setting lights and moving cameras. The chairs in the audience were still empty. I liked that "WOW" feeling of "this is television." I'd walk over to my podium and microphone, which was right on the stage. It was positioned to the left of the set where I was able to talk directly to the audience sitting below me and also to Alan Thicke, the producers, and the contestants.

I learned very quickly that warm-up is an art and can be very difficult to master — especially when a show is run like "Pictionary" was. I stayed on stage during the taping of the show and remained on stage after each one, while the rest of the cast left to go back to their dressing rooms to relax and change their wardrobe. I was still out there talking and talking and talking to the audience, before the next taping began. I was there for the next show and continued to entertain the audience until after the following show. That was five shows a day, five warm-ups, warm-downs, warm-arounds and five shows to announce. I never left the stage. I had to keep that audience entertained, because if anyone got bored that was trouble. Producers do not want a bored audience. If they weren't amped up to laugh at the jokes or applaud for the game, we would end up with a flat show. There was one audience for the first three shows of the day, then those folks would be released and the cast and crew took a lunch break. While we ate something quick, the next audience filed in for the last two shows of the day.

In between each show, I had 30 minutes to chat up the crowd of about 125 people. I did trivia contests, interviews, guessing games, impersonations, and then I'd look at my watch and realize I still had 20 more minutes to fill. Good God, what the hell do I do to keep these people engaged, happy, entertained? I started doing a talent show with audience members and that got me through a lot of those long waits between shows. People came up on stage, I'd interview them, find out what their talent was, they'd perform in front of everyone, and then at the end we'd have the audience applaud to pick the winner. The prize was usually a T-shirt or a mug from the show.

At the end of the day I was worn out. My voice was practically gone and I could barely get through dinner without doing a face-plant into my soup. I think warm-up is a great job for an up-and-coming comedian. I'm pretty sure if I only had to do two or three shows a day, I would have been all right. But being on the set performing all day, nonstop, and filling so much time by myself was challenging.

One of the producers of the show took pity on me. Mark Maxwell Smith is funny as the day is long, a real student of game shows and before he became a producer, Mark had been a warm-up guy. In my mind, he embodied the sensibility of a Borscht Belt comedian, someone who could have performed in those Catskills resorts. You know the style of humor, right? "Take my wife, please!" His delivery, his jokes, and the technique, all of it was great. Our stage manager was a man named Seth Mellman. Mark used to run all over the stage doing a perfect Jerry Lewis impersonation, stepping over footstools and onto sofas, yelling a la the famous comedian, "Seth MELL-MANN with the oy and the vey and hello laydieeee."

Every once in a while, Mark did the 30-minute routine for me between shows, so I could sit down. But he was so good,

I never even went back to my dressing room. I watched him from the side of the stage while I snacked on an apple. He had it down. Jokes that he used over and over again and that was one of the tricks of the trade. You can do the same stuff every tape day because there's always a new audience and he had a good 30 minutes of comedy bits. He had a sketch where he would say that the producers are so thankful for all of the audience members for taking the time from their day to be here with us. Then he said, "The producers have gifts for each and every one of you." The audience would hoot and applaud. He told everyone, "We've taped your prize to the bottom of your chair and if you would just reach under your seat…" One hundred twenty five people would bend over and reach under their theater chairs and Mark would say, "Under there you will find…" People would use their fingers to explore the underside of their chairs for their surprise and Mark would say, "You'll find an old chewed-up piece of gum." The audience reacted by jerking their hands back and with a chorus of "YUCKS," they all laughed and loved the trick played on them.

Mark also did a bit where he'd find a cute kid from the audience and bring him up on stage to interview him. It was always a sweet little interview where Mark would ask him about his family, his siblings, his mommy and daddy, and Mark would make some jokes about what the kid said. One time this kid didn't like the jokes Mark was making at his expense and this little eight-year-old boy hauled off and belted Mark right in the face with the biggest roundhouse punch you've ever seen. Mark was crouched down at the kid's level and was knocked right off his feet, onto his ass. Mark was surprised, everyone was, and it looked as if Mark was gonna grab this snotty-nosed kid by the collar and smack him right back. But he caught himself and brushed off some imaginary dust from the front of the kid's shirt, then sent him back to his parents in the audience. He got up and tossed the

mic to me to take over. Mark wasn't so eager to help out with my warm-ups after that.

I witnessed a few tussles between Alan and the producers and even the wardrobe staff. He once barged out of his dressing room with a handful of shirts, slacks, and sweaters, and started throwing them all over the set with the wardrobe staff scurrying after him, scooping it all up while he complained that it was all crap, and he was unable to wear any of it. It seemed to me he wanted Armani and apparently that wasn't in the budget. As he stormed off the set, one of the staff muttered, "Will someone let Alan know we're a game show, not the fucking Academy Awards."

As a fan of Alan Thicke, I felt I knew where he was coming from with the "edge" he had to him. Even so, I thought he could be a little demanding. And let's face it, to do what he does, you gotta have a pretty healthy ego as well. He was the host, the spotlight was on him and as far as I was concerned, he was "the man" and as the star, entitled to that position. I was just the announcer, but I was hoping for a little camaraderie, a little fun, only that wasn't going to happen with him.

Eventually it was my turn to take the heat. Mark Maxwell Smith wrote all the opening lines for the show. It was fun for me because Mark is smart and he wrote some great material for me to use when I introduced the contestants. The show always started cold, with the two contestants at the drawing board. The bouncy "Pictionary" music started playing and I'd have a funny line to say for each person as they drew something on the board. After the joke, I'd give their name and they would turn around to wave to the camera. Cute opening. I can't remember the line that ended it all, but it was particularly funny. The audience roared and then I introduced Alan as always with, "And here's yourrrr host of 'Pictionary'...Allllllan Thicke!!" Everyone applauded when Alan walked out and the first thing he said was something about the

announcer, Joe Cipriano, getting the funny line. He glanced over to the producer's table to ask why no one was writing the funny for him? I didn't think much of it at the time, in fact I was glad Alan thought I delivered a funny line, but after that taping my job definitely changed. My comedy days were over. From then on we had a new intro to the show that went like this:

Bouncy "Pictionary" Music starts:

Joe: "Welcome to 'Pictionary.' And now here's your host Alannnn Thicke."

Then Alan came out and said a funny line.

After "Pictionary" wrapped I'm guessing Alan Thicke went on to bewilder different producers, production assistants, and wardrobe people on other shows. Still, he was so darn charming on the air. Plus, Alan treated all of the guest stars with respect. And considering that there was a very mixed bag of celebrities, it showed me that Alan was a true performer.

The list of celebrity guest stars on "Pictionary" included Rosie O'Donnell, Weird Al Yankovic, Melba Moore, Ben Stein, Geraldo Rivera, and many more, but the most memorable show of all featured Erik Estrada and Bill Maher. It happened on October 3, 1997. First of all, when would you ever expect to see those two men on stage together, let alone on the same team on a game show? My impression of Bill was that he must have been wondering how in the world he landed on that show. To me he seemed somewhat annoyed to be there, but I have to tell you, he was a trouper. He was already gaining respect as the host of "Politically Incorrect." An intellectual with humor and here he was on "Pictionary" with Erik Estrada, not exactly known as an intellectual humorist or as a comedian. On the other hand, my impression of Erik Estrada was that he was thrilled to be on a game show, which is exactly the kind of personality you want

for that kind of program. So, with that in mind, the dynamic was: Erik is very amped, Bill is somewhat dragging his feet.

About halfway into the show they were doing a three-minute rapid-fire team round. Three members per team, two celebs and the contestant answered as many puzzles as possible within the allotted time. When a clue was guessed correctly, the next member on the team would rush to the board. People were jumping up, running to the board, running back to the sofa, sometimes kneeling on the floor. It was fast-paced and the perfect storm for the escalating excitement of the very excitable Erik Estrada. Each clue they got right, Erik got more animated. He ran to the board shouting and screaming, Bill ran to the board, the contestant ran to the board. At one point, the contestant was at the board drawing, Bill was on the sofa, and Estrada was kneeling on the floor beneath him. Erik got the phrase correct, "Tie a yellow ribbon 'round the old oak tree," he screamed. Alan said, "YES," and Bill started to get up off the sofa to get to the board. Erik, who had been kneeling on the floor, was apoplectic that he got the correct answer, so he celebrated by punching his fists into the air in a Rocky Balboa move. At that exact moment Bill Maher leaned forward to get off the couch, as Estrada's left fist met with Bill's nose and Bill Maher dropped like a rock to the floor. He was out for the count. The audience let out an audible gasp. The bouncy "Pictionary" music continued to play…the contestant tried to pull Bill up so he could win more money before the three minutes were up, but Bill was not moving. The music kept playing. Estrada was standing next to Alan nervously laughing as he explained to Alan, who had missed the action, what just happened.

I looked over at the producer's table and each one had a hand up to their mouth in shock. The audience had their hands up to their faces, too. The music continued to play but it seemed to slow down. I was told that really didn't happen but it felt like it in my

head. Looking back at the shocked faces, Bill splayed out on his back, I thought everything sllowwwwed down. Then the audio engineer stopped the music completely and the room was quiet. Suddenly everyone rushed to Bill. By this time he had regained consciousness and held onto his nose. He stood up and pointed a bloody finger at Estrada and I thought I heard him whimper something about calling his agent, then he rushed off the stage.

Paramedics tended to Bill in his dressing room and I was hit in the nose with an extra half hour of keeping the audience entertained. I went through every joke I had ever used in my life. You never really understand how long a half hour is until you have to fill it. By the time they were ready to start up the show, I had nothing left to say and was thrilled to be finished with my last warm-up of the day.

Bill came out dabbing at his nose with a tissue and the cast came out dressed in various forms of boxing attire. It was pretty funny. Even Bill couldn't keep from laughing. After the next commercial break, Bill had a Band-Aid on his nose and everyone else on stage had one on his or her nose as well. For the rest of the show, Estrada kept away from Maher and we finished up then everyone went home to crash and be back the next day for five more.

Working on "Pictionary" was a great experience. I finally got to do a game show in Studio Thirty-three at CBS Television City. It was a kick, what you might call a bucket list item. I've seen Alan several times since then and I doubt he even remembers who the hell I am, but he's always been very nice to me. Mark Maxwell Smith is still funny and Studio Thirty-three is still going strong. In fact, these days when they're not taping the "Price is Right" on that stage, believe it or not, that's where they tape a show called "Real Time with Bill Maher." I wonder if Bill ever made the connection?

JOE-DAVE-JIM-BOB-BOY

I've been called a lot of names in my lifetime, a few I don't want to repeat. Most of them you already know. Stoney, from WKYS, calls me Joe. Another one of my best friends, John, calls me Dave. I've got buddies from WWCO who still call me Tommy or Collins. Uncle Johnny, from C-O and Q107, calls me Kid, our nickname for one another. Then there's Susan Berman Moore, a vice president at FOX. I've known Susan for more than 25 years. She knows my real name is David but she said I will always be Joe to her. She recently told me, "You don't look like a Dave. I could never call you that." One of the kids from our Palisades neighborhood, Cassie Green, calls me Poppa Joe. When I was on the air at KKHR, I was Dave, but my last name was Donovan.

All of these names can be rather confusing. Not just for Ann and me but also for our friends. One of Ann's good friends from KABC-TV in L.A. came up with an unusual solution for all of my names. That was Susan Norris, now Susan Porcaro Goings, a television reporter and anchor for Channel Seven. Susan started calling me Joe-Dave-Jim-Bob-Boy and it stuck. Most of Ann's friends from work still call me that. Good thing I'm not a football player because I don't think there's enough room on a jersey to stitch all my names on the back.

It's a silly predicament having all these different names, but I've gotten used to it over the years. When I first met Ann I

introduced myself as Joe and that's what she called me until she met my family. Since my mom called me Dave, Ann decided that's the name she would use too. When we moved to Los Angeles it was a new start in a new city. I suppose I could have picked any name I wanted, but I had gotten used to the name Joe. Once we had kids, it got more complicated.

We had been married for five years and I knew Ann was ready to start a family. One night she got me drunk and took advantage of me. The next thing I knew we were having a baby. At least that's my story and I'm sticking to it.

It was time to move out of that tiny house in the Palisades and Ann found the perfect one just about one mile away. When she walked in to see it for the first time, it was empty. Workmen were busy putting a fresh coat of white paint everywhere. There was a radio sitting on the mantel in the living room turned up loud and one of her favorite songs was echoing through the empty house, "Time After Time," by Cyndi Lauper. As the song ended, the disc jockey came on and it was me. One of me, anyway. The station was KKHR where I was Dave Donovan. It seemed like fate. The house sat back on a bluff, overlooking the Pacific Ocean, on a quiet street in the Palisades. Turn your head one way and you looked right down onto a sandy beach, look the other way and you could see the Santa Monica Mountains. Of course we couldn't afford it, the loan was huge, and with interest rates at about 15 percent back then, I brown-bagged it to work for a long time. The neighborhood seemed like it was right out of one of those old fifties TV shows like "Leave It to Beaver" or "Ozzie and Harriet." There were two streets that curved to meet at both ends, forming a loop. We thought it was the perfect place to bring up a family. Buying that house turned out to be the best use of money I didn't have.

Our daughter Dayna was born four months after we moved in to our new home. She was three weeks early and we were still

fixing up her room when she decided to make her entrance. Like many people, I was completely unprepared for the unexpected joy our little girl would bring to our lives. She has a thousand-watt smile and a big heart to match. She will always be my baby girl. Two and a half years later, our son Alex came into the world. Determined to beat Dayna's early appearance, he was two months premature. The whole experience scared the hell out of me and thankfully, mom and son were fine. He stayed in the hospital for a couple of weeks after Ann came home. I went to see him every day, sat by his incubator in the neonatal intensive care unit, with his tiny little hand wrapped around my pinkie. I knew he was going to be a great guy. My brother Henry was named after our dad and I thought about doing the same thing with our son, but which name would we use? Joe or Dave? I always felt I hadn't treated my given name with enough respect and I wanted to honor what my parents chose for me, so we passed my name on to our only son as his middle name. Alex David came home to us two weeks after he was born, healthy and strong.

I can't say enough about how much I love our kids and how grateful I am to have these two people in my life. Bringing up my own family gave me perspective on the roller-coaster world where I worked. It also introduced me to a whole new family of friends, people from our neighborhood who didn't know anything about voice-overs. Since our street formed a loop, we called ourselves The Loop Group. John and Deborah Lloyd, Peter and Patti Black, Russ and Elisa Hunziker, George and Dana Zaloom, Tracy and Christian Williams, Peggy and Richard McLaughlin. Our kids are like cousins. We celebrate every holiday together, take vacations together, share birthdays and dinners. When we had to fill out emergency forms at our kids' schools, we didn't have any family near-by to put down on those documents. Our neighborhood friends' names were the ones that went on that list. Years later, when Peter Black died suddenly, just 50 years old, I gave the

eulogy at his funeral, surrounded by our family of friends and half of Pacific Palisades. In 2013 when Peter's oldest daughter Cassie got married, she and her fiancé, Josh Green, asked me to perform their wedding ceremony. Reverend Joe Dave Jim Bob Boy.

Our group has grown to include Lisa Plonsker, Kelly Anderson, Kathy Smith, and Susan and Drew Gitlin. Since not everyone lives on the Loop anymore, and some never did, now we say the "Loop" is a state of mind, rather than a location. To this day, every Monday a text goes out to the group and whoever is available meets at Pearl Dragon restaurant in the Palisades for dinner. It's a special gathering of friends who all call me Dave, or Davey Cip. Except for John. He sometimes calls me Young Dave. Go figure.

John Lloyd is my closest friend, probably because we shared so many of the same experiences growing up. He was born just three weeks before me, in Leigh-on-Sea in Great Britain. He is a world-class athlete, a professional tennis player. In his day he was number one in Britain, number 21 in the world, and a star on the British Davis Cup Team. Did I say we have a lot in common? Okay, so where's the shared experience? None of that stuff is the same but we're getting to it now.

John knew what he was going to do with his life when he was just a kid. Like me, neither one of us went to college. We were too busy working, to take time out for school. We weren't exactly model students, anyway. We are both self-made men who had to rely on our talent for work. His in tennis, mine in broadcasting. As a teenager, John took the train from his small hometown to get to endless practices and matches. I took the bus from Oakville to 65 Bank Street to learn about radio. We both had success early in our lives, at just 16 years old. By the time we both turned 20, John was already number one in the UK and I had made it to major-market radio. All right, it's obvious John is much more talented than I am, but I got the good looks. Oh crap, that's not true, either.

I'm not sure what kind of influence I've had on John, but he definitely inspired me to take up tennis. I absolutely love the game. I didn't pick up a racket until I was 40 years old and now you nearly have to pry it out of my hands to get me off the court.

When I hit the big four-oh I realized I needed more balance in my life. In my twenties, it seemed life was all about my career, how far could I go and how fast could I get there. In my thirties, it was about family. Now it was time to take care of myself, get some exercise, make sure I would be in good shape to enjoy my job and my kids. What's important about playing a good tennis game also translates into my career. You're not likely to have any success on the court if you don't have good form, if you don't practice. During a game sometimes, there's an impulse to end the point early but that can lead to a miss-hit into the net, or outside the lines. Patience. Hit your shots, wait for your opening, then go for the winner. Same thing with voice-over. Most likely, you won't start booking gigs right off the bat. Take workshops, seminars, hone your talent. Increase your confidence. Over the years I have worked with voice coaches, including Marice Tobias, in L.A. She's helped me several times with refining my delivery. Once when I told her I was having difficulty switching from my comedy read at FOX to a heavy drama read at NBC, she had an idea that worked perfectly for me. She told me to change my clothes according to what network I was working for at that particular time. If I started the day at FOX, that meant I was doing a comedy promo. I wore my regular jeans, or shorts, and a casual shirt. If I was booked to do a heavy drama at NBC later in the day, I changed into an all-black wardrobe, nice slacks and a button-down shirt. It was visual cue that helped me alter my mood. A smart trick from a knowledgeable friend. Working with a coach is one way to continue to learn about the business and find out where you fit into the mix. Keep moving forward, stay on the balls of your feet, ready to react in an instant.

I play tennis at least three times a week, more if I can find a game. These days I'm about a four-point-oh player which is average to pretty good. I can keep up with just about anyone, hang in long enough to make it a good game and get some decent exercise. Oh, and thank you Mark Miller for giving me a forehand. I like to win but for me, it's more about having fun, playing well, and spending time with my friends. Did I already say I like to win?

Because of our friendship with Deb and John and their kids Aiden and Hayley, our families have gone on some fantastic trips together, often centering on tennis. We've been fortunate enough to go to Wimbledon, the U.S. Open, and even Barbados where I was the chair umpire for a charity match between John, Aiden, John's brother David and his son Scott. That was a blast. One of our best vacations ever.

I was chair umpire one other time, for another charity exhibition. It happened in the Palisades between John and his longtime friend, tennis great Jimmy Connors. There were actually two of those tall umpire chairs on the court, side by side. My co-umpire was another Palisadian, actor and comedian Martin Short. This was not a serious event. Every time John prepared to serve, as soon as he tossed up the ball, I asked Martin a question. That is horrible tennis etiquette. I did it to Jimmy, too.

John goes to serve. "Play much tennis in Canada, Martin?" I asked.

John is distracted and misses his serve.

"Yes, there is a window of about three hours in August when we all hit the courts," Martin said.

During one of Connors's tosses, Martin golf whispered into the microphone, "Look at Connors. He looks so young. His cheeks are smooth and taut."

I hit back with, "Yes, all four of them."

Connors about fell over.

Martin looked at me and in all honesty said, "Who are you? And why are you here?"

I said, "I have no idea. When I arrived, this was the only empty chair in the place, so I took it."

By far, one of my favorite tennis events to attend was the Seniors Championship in London. It takes place in December, when the city is dressed up for the holidays. I went for the first time with John, in 2003. The matches are played at the Royal Albert Hall, a beautiful building filled with history. Famous entertainers and politicians have appeared at the Hall since it opened in 1871, including Winston Churchill, Nelson Mandela, Frank Sinatra, The Beatles, Eric Clapton, and more recently, the singer Adele. It's the same building John Lennon sang about in his song, "A Day In The Life."

This is a fun event because you get the likes of Jim Currier, John McEnroe, Matts Wilander, and so many others, but you also get to see many of the legends of the game compete, like Henri Leconte, Ilie Nastase, Johan Kriek, and my buddy John Lloyd. Those matches are the most fun to watch because the players are so incredibly talented they can do just about anything with the tennis ball. The games are light, and they are played for comedy and entertainment, as much as for a win. John not only played in the doubles matches but he also called the games for BBC Television.

There are two tennis sessions a day during the Albert Hall tournament and between the day and evening matches we would go out to dinner with friends and other players, then come back so John could either play in a doubles match or do the color

commentary for BBC. On this one occasion, we had gone to one of John's favorite restaurant's in London called Hush, then grabbed a black cab for the ride back to Albert Hall. When we walked into the players' entrance, we saw a very dapper gentleman talking to one of the security officers. He had on a long, dark cashmere coat with a beautiful scarf draped over his shoulders. Immediately we realized it was the legendary singer Tony Bennett. Mister Bennett is a huge tennis fan and he recognized John right away.

"John, is there any way you can help me get downstairs into the locker room?" he wondered in that beautiful voice. "I want to wish John McEnroe good luck tonight before his match."

"Of course," John said. Then he turned to the security man and said, "I'll take Mister Bennett downstairs."

As we walked towards the locker room, I had a funny thought rolling around in my head. I had met Tony Bennett once before, and this chance encounter was too perfect not to bring it up. To get to that story, we need to go back in time, for a little background information.

It was February of 2000 and our little family had just moved from Pacific Palisades to a beautiful old home in Beverly Hills. We didn't want to leave the Loop, but that perfect house on the bluff, overlooking the ocean, turned out to be a bit of bad luck. Two years earlier, there was a particularly bad rainy season in Los Angeles, the first time I ever heard the weather term "El Niño." The overwhelming amount of rain created geological havoc and there was a landslide at the base of the canyon that threatened our home up top. What started as a tiny crack in the ground, from the corner of our house to the edge of the bluff, turned into a 30-foot drop in one month. It still hurts to talk about it. We lost a portion of the backyard and half of our big beautiful deck that looked down to the sandy beach below. Amazingly, the house remained

structurally sound. Still, we had to hire a contractor, soils experts, and a geological engineer to figure out how to stabilize the slide from further damage. In the end, after many long talks, Ann told me, whenever it rained, she would never again feel safe in our home. We made the difficult decision to move.

We had lived in that house for 18 years and didn't make a penny when we sold it. A contractor bought it from us for the cost of the remaining mortgage. Eighteen years of property appreciation slid right down the hill with the dirt. We wanted to stay as close as possible to our friends, and ended up in Beverly Hills. I never imagined that one day I would make my home in the famous 90210 zip code. More than ten years of working in voice-over helped us qualify for that mortgage. Once again, we tightened our financial belts to swing the deal and in exchange we wound up in my dream home, a house that had a pool and a tennis court. At least once a month, the Loop Group came over for a full day of food, tennis, and swimming, a throwback to those days my mom and dad had their house full of family and friends on Sunday afternoons. No bocce or baseball this time. We played tennis and ping-pong, and went swimming. My buddy Russ called our place "the Cipriano Tennis and Aquatic Center." After the misery of the landslide, the neighborhood we ended up in was an unintended treat, especially for me.

We loved living in Beverly Hills. What's not to like? Since I am a little bit of a Hollywood history geek, it was a thrill for me to see the homes where famous television and movie stars once raised their kids and lived their lives. There is one street in particular, probably more than any other street in the world, where many legendary celebrities lived all at the same time. That street is Roxbury Drive. When we moved to Beverly Hills, we ended up right around the corner from that stretch of road, one block away. I walked our dog on that street nearly every day, past

the homes where so many talented and creative people once lived. Lucille Ball, Jimmy Stewart, one of my favorites Jack Benny, along with Peter Falk, George Gershwin, Ira Gershwin, Jeanne Crain, Agnes Moorehead, the list goes on and on. Diane Keaton had just sold her home on Roxbury Drive to Madonna when we moved in around the corner onto Chevy Chase Drive. My buddy Sandy Grushow bought a house on Roxbury and raised his children there as well. Our house backed up to a beautiful estate owned by the late, great Rosemary Clooney. Hang on, we're almost to the point of the story.

Two of the most extraordinary voice-over talents I have ever had the pleasure to know are brothers Miguel and Rafael Ferrer. Their parents were Rosemary Clooney and José Ferrer. If you don't know who those two people are, you are missing out on Hollywood history. Do yourself a favor and Google them both, right now. Miguel's sound is one of my all-time favorite voices, clear, pure, and deep. Rafael's voice is just as beautiful, but different. His sound is rough, rugged, and gets down there in the dirt and gravel. We had been friends for a few years, when Ann and I moved to Beverly Hills, across the alley from their family home. I used to see them in the neighborhood and at work.

Their beloved mom, Rosemary, died in June 2002 and a couple of months later her family held a beautiful tribute concert in her honor at the Beverly Hilton Hotel. Ann and I were pleased to be invited, to support our friends Miguel and Raffy. The tribute included performances by kd Lang, Rosemary's daughter-in-law Debbie Boone, Merv Griffin, her nephew George Clooney, and so many others, including, yes, Tony Bennett. Ahhh, now you see where we're going!

At one point during the night, I went to use the bathroom. At first I thought it was empty, but as I turned the corner for the urinal, there was Mister Bennett, stepping up as well.

"Beautiful memorial," I said. Zip.

"It is," he said. Zip. With a twinkle in his eye that said to me, yes, you're taking a piss with Tony Bennett.

We both finished our business, washed up, then went back into the ballroom. End of story. Until one year later, at Royal Albert Hall. As we walked Tony Bennett to McEnroe's locker room I couldn't resist.

"Mister Bennett. It's nice to see you, but actually, we've met before," I said.

"Oh?"

"Yes," I said. "You and I once shared a pee at the Beverly Hilton Hotel."

Without missing a beat he said, "Really? Was it in the swimming pool?"

The stunned look on my face, and the smirk on Tony Bennett's face nearly dropped John to the floor, laughing. I was being a wise-ass and I'm not sure how I expected him to react, but his timing and sense of humor were flawless. When we delivered Mister Bennett to McEnroe, Tony hoisted a thumb in my direction and told Mac, "I took a pee with this one!"

The joke was lost on McEnroe but John and I were left in tears, laughing our way out the door.

The following year we were back in London for the same event. All of the players were staying at a very nice hotel called The Carlton Towers, and John had gotten me a discounted rate as a family friend. The second night we were there, we had gone to dinner and then to the night matches and at the end of a long day John was tired. At 11 o'clock he went to bed and I went up

to the rooftop bar for a nightcap. Several of the players were there and they invited me to join in their conversation.

At about midnight, I headed down to my room on the fourth floor and slipped my card key into the lock. I had walked into my room, set my wallet on the bench by the door, when I sensed movement in the room. Someone was sleeping in my bed, and it wasn't Goldilocks. I inched closer and saw there was most definitely a man in my bed. Under my covers. Well, actually he was half under my covers. He had one leg in and one leg out and he wasn't wearing any pants. By the way, when I told this story to the folks in London, I learned that "not wearing any pants" meant he wasn't wearing any underwear. My English friends corrected me. What I should have said is, "He wasn't wearing any trousers." Trousers, pants whatever, there was a guy in my bed at midnight and he stirred as I walked into the room. I did a double-take look at my key, as if I could tell if I was in the wrong room by checking a generic plastic card. That's when he started to wake up.

"Whosh there?" he said, lifting his wet, drooling face off of my pillow.

"Who's there??" I said. "Who the hell are you?"

"Huh, whatzamattah?" My new roommate tried to get up but he was way beyond three sheets to the wind, he was on his fourth or fifth sheet, and they were MY sheets, by the way.

Crap, I thought. What the hell do I do now?

"How did you get into my room and WHY are you in my room?" I asked, a little louder than I intended.

"Wait, hold on fella, yer in MY room!"

"I'm not in your room, look at the computer on the desk over there, that's MY computer."

He stumbled out of my bed and headed to the desk and slurred, "You wait! I'll getta the bottom of thish."

He picked up my phone on my desk and pressed "0." The front desk answered and my roommate said, "Skoosh me, but ham I calling you from my room?"

He looked back at me through bleary eyes and said as he covered the mouthpiece of the phone, "She sez I'm in my room."

"Gimme the phone," I said. It was beginning to feel like a "Three Stooges" movie.

"Hello, this is Mr. Cipriano in room 424. I just walked into my room and found this strange man in my bed."

"There is a man in your bed, sir??" the front desk person answered.

"Yes, can you send someone up here to help me sort this out?"

"Yes, right away Mr. Cipriano." I think this is when the hotel's "oh shit" alarm went off.

At this point my new roommate was beginning to come 'round to the fact that something wasn't right. He had been pretty sure up to now that he was in his room and I was an uninvited guest, but now as his head cleared and he saw that everything in the room did not belong to him, he began to search his well-pickled memory to determine just how he ended up in someone else's room.

That's when I noticed that the connecting doors between our two rooms were opened. Mystery solved. Those pass-through doors must not have been locked and in his inebriated state, he probably stumbled into my room on his way to the loo. I also

found there was "evidence" he had used my loo, uh bathroom, as well and I didn't even want to look at my toothbrush. I just tossed it into the trashcan. While I checked out the rest of the stuff, he stumbled through the door into to his own room, slid under his covers, probably hoping this was just a bad dream.

At that moment there was a knock on my door. I opened it to find two very big security guys outside. I recapped the story to them, told them the situation with the connecting doors, and while one went into the hallway to knock on my neighbor's door, the other stayed with me. Now what? I said, "I'm sorry, but I'm not going to get in this bed after that strange dude slept there, with his face on my pillow and the rest of him under my covers. Can we please call housekeeping to send up new bed sheets and pillowcases?"

He called down only to find out that housekeeping was long gone. It ended up that my two big security guys went downstairs, got linens, and came up and made my bed themselves. I was extremely impressed and told them so. They even got the corners right.

Before going to sleep, I took a bungee cord that I had used on my luggage, wrapped it around the handle of the common door, then pulled it tight, securing it to my closet door. I thought there was no way I was going to risk letting that guy stumble back into my bed while I was in it, sleeping.

As I turned off the light that night, I wondered if I should make a fuss about this with the manager of the hotel. But since I was staying there as a friend of John's, I decided to just leave it alone. I didn't want to make waves.

The next morning, I was just about to head downstairs for

breakfast and buy a new toothbrush, when the phone rang. It was the hotel manager, apologizing profusely for last night's embarrassing developments. Apparently the two big security guys had filed a report. I wonder how many times they laughed during the writing of such a ridiculous story. The manager asked to see me in person. Five minutes later, a very proper woman appeared at my door and introduced herself as the manager. She apologized again and asked me how she could make up for my unfortunate experience. I really didn't think it was that bad after all, no harm, no foul, and I said it wasn't necessary.

"Of course it is," she said. "Please allow me to upgrade your room."

Okay, twist my arm a little more. Yes, you may upgrade my room.

She asked me to follow her so she could show me a room that might be more to my liking. We walked into the elevator and she pressed the button for the penthouse floor. I think I may have giggled out loud, but maybe not. I'd like to think I was a little more composed than that.

As we got off the lift I noticed the floor was all just a little bit nicer. The carpet was thicker, the doors to each room were larger, it was even quieter. The paintings on the wall were of dukes and duchesses and damsels and whatever other word starts with "D." It was all very British.

At the end of the hall, we paused at a double-door entrance, she pulled out a gold key, not a plastic card, and unlocked the door. She pushed open the doors, revealing a beautiful marble foyer that welcomed you into an expansive living room, which she called "the lounge." To the right was a master bedroom that

was huge, and a closet that was bigger than my room downstairs. The bathroom was absolutely epic.

"Do you think this will make up for your unfortunate experience?" she asked.

"Uh, yep," I think I said. Perhaps I was more eloquent, but I doubt it.

She handed me the key and said the butler would bring up my belongings within the hour.

"Butler?"

"Yes, every suite on this floor is butled."

"Butled? Ohhh kayyy."

She shook my hand and breezed out the double doors. I walked into the lounge with the gold key in my hand and the word "butled" buzzing round my head. I stepped up to the window to take in the most amazing view of the city, including the London Eye, that huge Ferris wheel on the banks of the River Thames.

My first thought was, "John is gonna crap when he sees this." And I ran to the phone.

"You're absolutely bloody kidding me?" he said as I welcomed him into my suite through the double doors.

"Bloody HELL," he said, then turned to his left and blurted out, "A bloody LOUNGE?" Huh, how about that. I guess they really do call their living room a lounge over here. "They gave you all this because a bloke was in your bed in his bloody underwear?" John says "bloody" a lot.

"Yeah. Oh and I have a butler."

John's voice went up another octave, "A BLOODY BUTLER??"

"Yeah, all of us here on this floor are butled."

When we got to the Albert Hall that day, John told everyone the story of "Dave and the bloke in his bed in his underwear." We were sitting in the basement of the Royal Albert Hall with the sponsors of the event and some of the players, including McEnroe's manager. They loved listening to John recount my day. Everyone laughed and they were quite impressed with my good fortune.

Mac's manager said, "Shit, I think that's bigger than McEnroe's suite." Later that day, between matches, he ran over to my room to have a look at it himself. "Shit, this IS bigger than Mac's suite." Then I called the butler to have him bring us some tea. I hate tea, but I didn't know what else to ask him for.

I had that penthouse suite for the rest of my stay, which was another five days. John spent every free moment in my lounge watching the telly and munching on crisps and things.

He looked up at me and said, "You've hit the bloody jackpot, you have."

And I had to agree. It sure did seem like I had hit the bloody jackpot. Not just in London, but back home too, with my family and friends. And it all came from a couple of random decisions and misfortunes. Moving to that house on the Loop, discovering new friends for life, enduring a landslide, picking up a tennis racket, finding a stranger in my bed, oh and taking a piss.

That's when I realized I had found some balance in my life. I didn't even know it had been missing. Up until now, almost every decision I made, from the time I was 14 years old, was all about work. It took me nearly 30 years to learn about what most people already know, how to take more time out for the simple pleasures in my life, just like my dad so many years ago. Most of it doesn't have anything to do with my job. It's all about my other life, the personal stuff, my friends, and family. My life as Dave Cipriano.

Call Me Lucky

As a young boy, when I dreamed about becoming a deejay, I had enough faith in myself that I was sure if I paid attention and worked hard, I could get a job at one of those powerhouse radio stations I listened to late at night. And that would have been good enough for me to be happy. I ended up with a career that I never even knew was an option. I had no idea what a voice-over was, or a promo. I didn't know they existed. Once I learned about that part of the business, I was inspired to find a job in network television. Funny enough, as I tried to break into voice-over work, it ended up finding me, back on the radio.

I was at KIIS-FM, doing any kind of job that was available, producing commercials, and filling in for the deejay's on vacation. I hadn't changed much from the days when I used to hang out at WWCO, running errands for the guys on the air. Now here I was, so many years later, doing nearly the same thing. I continued to create opportunities for new advantages to open up in my life. And that's when Bob Bibb at FOX-TV heard me on KIIS-FM. I believe if people think positively and visualize their goals coming true, you can make your own good fortune. I think I've been lucky that way.

The voice-over business has changed dramatically since 1988, when I did my first promo for FOX television. I used to put a lot of miles on my car, driving from session to session. And I used

to spend invaluable time with other voice actors, hanging out at all the different studios, while we waited our turn to go into the audio booth.

Technology changed all of that. I was one of the first to embrace the new advances in telecommunications. I did it because I love electronics, computers, all of the toys that come with professional mechanical gadgets. I did it so I could spend more time with my family, without having to run out after dinner for a late-night session. I did it so I could tuck my kids into bed at night.

My dad helped me build my first real studio. Not the one I put together with duct tape and a plastic turntable. No, the one we built was several steps up from that. For my thirtieth birthday, Annie surprised me with a Neumann U87 microphone, and then told me to build a studio around it. Of course I always listen to my wife so that's what I did. We were living in our house on the Loop in the Palisades and there was a little room tucked under the kitchen that we could get to from the outside.

My dad and I drew up a rough blueprint, framed the room, and added a window with a view of the ocean that I could look out of from my chair. When we needed an extra hand, Ann helped install the wallboard while my mom kept an eye on our kids. It was a family project. When we were done, it wasn't exactly soundproof, but it was good enough. I could still hear plenty of what was going on above my head in the house, even the clicking sound from our dog's nails as he walked across the kitchen tiles. Whenever I had to record something, I yelled upstairs for everyone to tiptoe around or please move to the other side of the house.

I did a ton of work from that little studio. When I was struggling to make ends meet, working part-time at KIIS-FM, I used to produce voice-over tapes for other people who wanted to break into the business. I also engineered a show for comedian Brad

Sanders called "Cla'nce and the All My Children Update." It was a funny, daily report about the most popular soap opera on TV at that time. I even did a Top 40 radio show from my studio that was broadcast in two cities in Japan, Tokyo and Yokohama. Produced by Debra Grant, it was all in English and ran for five years. But when it came to network promos and voice-overs we all still drove to the individual studios. I miss those personal connections.

Nowadays, nearly every voiceover actor has his or her own studio at home, myself included. I call it the "clubhouse," kind of a throw back to those days at WWCO. And so is the booth. It's designed by George Whittam with floating walls, thick double doors, and a digital control board. It's set up like a radio studio because that's how I feel most comfortable. There's even a glass window that looks out from the studio into the rest of my office. It's so airtight I've been able to record a session with a helicopter flying above the house.

Because many of us have our own studios, most voiceover actors are secluded from one another and the people who work at the networks and production companies. I think it's important to make an effort to keep those relationships alive. Some of my closest friends are the producers, writers, and editors who work on trailers and promos. For me, it's all about face-to-face contact. That's what gives our business its heart. My voice-over colleagues are also my friends. They are not my competition. Sure, many of us audition for the same jobs, but together we are a group of people with shared goals with whom we can celebrate our successes and commiserate over our failures. We strive to make our dreams come true by standing on each other's shoulders to lend a helping hand.

Since we no longer see one another on a daily basis and in fact we may go months without any contact at all, I'm always looking for reasons for us to get together. One of those turned out to be

the creation of the Don LaFontaine Voice-Over Lab at the SAG Foundation. Don's best friend Paul Pape asked me to help build the lab, along with other actors in the voice over community. Together we dug deep into our pockets to make that dream a reality. Today the Lab is thriving and providing free workshops and seminars to anyone who is interested in pursuing a career in voice-over. The state-of-the-art studios are available free of charge for actors to work on their craft, book studio time to record auditions, or just get on a microphone and do what I used to do in that little studio at WWCO in Waterbury, Connecticut. You have to get inside an audio booth and experiment in order to learn. At this time, I'm pleased to say, there's another lab under construction at SAG Foundation headquarters in New York.

I've had my share of good fortune in life so I'm happy to donate my time for a worthy cause. That's one of the reasons why the Primetime Voices for Children was created. A few years ago, I reached out to many of my colleagues in voice-over to ask them to record a couple of lines from the holiday poem "'Twas the Night Before Christmas." Thirty-one people responded! They all sent me their lines and I carefully edited them together, making sure to include each and every actor. John Masecar from Astral Communications in Vancouver took the voice track I sent him and produced it with music and sound effects. We sold it on iTunes and CD Baby with all the proceeds going to the Mattel Children's Hospital at UCLA, where Ann volunteers. One week before Christmas a bunch of us met at the Child Life Center to read stories to the kids who couldn't go home for Christmas. That year we raised over $7,000 for the hospital.

I got the gang together again the following year, to record a full album of children's stories. This time we added all original music composed by my friend Greg Chun. We released, "'Twas the Night Before Christmas and other Classic Children's Stories"

in December of 2012 and again all proceeds went to the hospital. Over 20 of us visited the kids, bringing toys along with the cash. I am proud to say that year we raised over $10,000. I hope it becomes an annual event.

To this day, I still work hard to make my own luck happen. Some people don't think I have to worry about that anymore, but truth be told, if I don't work, I don't get paid. Voice-over is fickle. All of us are at the whim of pop culture and changing styles. A voice that worked in 2012 might not work five years later because tastes change, marketing strategies change, and new talent fills the void. Depending on my voice to make a living is not easy. I've had my share of sleepless nights, wondering when I was going to book my next gig. So when someone says to me "you're a shoo-in for this job" or "that's a sure thing," in my experience, I never believe it. I've lost more "sure things" than my broken heart will allow me to remember. And that's probably a better way to look at life. I end up not taking any gig for granted. I thoroughly and honestly enjoy each new job, and celebrate the wins. I try to see all the possibilities in each opportunity.

The career I chose is a roller coaster, and I hate roller coasters. But I love what I do and wouldn't change it for anything. Even though I know that free fall could be waiting for me just around the bend, when you take that ride with people you love, something wonderful happens.

I was just a kid when I walked through the doors of 65 Bank Street and made some life long friends. I have wonderful memories of that time and a grateful feeling of thanks to those people who helped me find my way, from Oakville, to Washington, D.C., to Los Angeles. There were so many generous friends who gave me a hand up when I needed it the most. I hope to be regarded as that same kind of person, the first to put out my hand to someone else who is looking for a boost. I think it's good for your heart.

You never know when your life is about to change, for better or worse. I try to be prepared for whatever comes my way. I want to be ready to take advantage of those special moments and will always hope for the best.

We were living in Beverly Hills when my neighbor called out to me one day. It was television producer Chuck Fries, godfather of the Movie of the Week. Leaning on his fence, watching me play tennis, he shouted out, "Look at you Cipriano, your own tennis court, a beautiful wife, and best of all you get to live right next door to me."

I laughed and said, "What can I say, Chuck, I'm a lucky guy."

Chuck replied, "Let me tell you something, Cip, Hollywood's little secret is that success is ninety percent luck and ten percent a lotta luck."

I believe he's right. With hard work and a lot of luck, I got to be good at what I do. Number one, I had the desire. Number two, I was willing to put in any amount of hours that were necessary. Number three, I had some sort of natural talent that lined up with my passion. Number four, probably most important, I got lucky.

I've had the good fortune to experience some wonderful moments in my life. Often, not because I think I deserved it, but because of the people I met along the way. For whatever reason, they invited me to join them on some very fun adventures.

I can't wait to see what's next.

Acknowledgements

There are so many people I've met along the way in my broadcasting and voice-over careers, as well as in my personal life, who became part of my story and are like family to me.

While writing this book, I received a lot of help from many of the people I worked with back when I was a teenager at WWCO in Waterbury, CT. People like Larry Rifkin, Tim Clark, Ron Gregory, Peter Marcus, Joe Sherwood, Danny Lyons, Bill Raymond, Steve Martin, and Johnny Walker (Paul Michaud) who were there with me.

I nervously sent my buddy Mike Holland the chapter about the two of us. He told me he loved it and couldn't wait to read the entire book, adding with a chuckle, "Wow, I was a little slut." He asked if I would consider including his real name, Michael Bouyea, since he no longer uses Holland. I was touched that he wanted his friends to know this was his story, too. I only wish I knew where Jerry Wolf is these days. If you happen to see him, please tell him how indebted I am to him for his generosity.

To my friends at WWCO, WDRC, WKYS, NBC in Washington, Q107, KHTZ, KKHR, and KIIS AM and FM, all of you have enriched my life in so many wonderful ways. Thanks to Louise Palanker, Todd Parker McLaren, and Ed Scarborough who helped bring to life many memories from the KIIS and KKHR radio days.

To all of the people at FOX, CBS, and NBC, the producers, audio mixers, and so many others at the various studios around town, some of you I don't see daily but I think of you often. I would like to name everyone but I'm worried I might accidently forget someone's name. Many of you have become close and dear friends. All of you have changed my life in the best way possible, both at work and on the tennis court.

I can't say enough about my voice-over colleagues. We really do support each other to help reach our goals, something I think we all learned from Don LaFontaine and we carry on that tradition to this day.

I've enjoyed a rare experience in the voice-over business; I've been with the same agents for more than twenty years. I couldn't have any better people looking out for my career. Thank you to Rita Vennari, president of SBV Talent Agency, Mary Ellen Lord and Jessica Bulavsky. They're my friends and even though they represent a lot of talent, they make it seem like I'm the only person in the world they're working for.

Thank you to our wonderful friends and relatives for supporting our efforts, the Loop Group, Janet Davis, Lauren Spiegel, Debbie and Malcolm Orrall, Vicki and Bruce Pate, Chuck Duran and Stacey Aswad, and Russ Suchala who keeps Annie and me fit and healthy. A big thanks to my dog, Sammy, for being my buddy in the studio every day. You're a good pal.

A few of our friends read portions of the book and made wonderful suggestions– Barbara Grieco, Kelly Anderson, and John and Deb Lloyd. It was also important for us to get feedback and guidance from our editor, Meghan Stevenson. Meghan has been encouraging and thoughtful in helping us tell this story. And thanks to our copy editor and proofreader, Marcia C. Abramson, and our cover designer, Velin Saramov, at Perseus Design. Thank

you to Marice Tobias for directing the audio book, AJ McKay for audio production, and Greg Chen for his original music.

To my family, my big brother Henry and his wife Eileen, a heartfelt thank you for your encouragement and support my entire life. To their children Christine and Mark, and their spouses Kurt and Skye, you are all great. Chris's two wonderful kids, Tyler and Ashlyn, give us such joy and a lotta laughs. Chris and Kurt, I apologize for taking your kids out at the crack of dawn for sugary, donut filled breakfasts. I just can't help myself. Thank you to Ann's family, her brother Andy, and her beautiful mom, Audrey, who loves her Catholic son-in-law unconditionally – I love you too, Grandma. Thank you to my sister-in-law Amy Gudelsky and Steven Schwartz and her two wonderful kids Eric and Zev and his wife, Sami. I have great-nieces on that side of the family as well, in the amazing Parker Rae who brightens up my day every time I see her smile and her brand-new sister Harley Skye.

I have two more very important people in my life who have given me great joy and huge amounts of love since the moment they were born. My beautiful daughter, Dayna Leigh, who is a successful public relations person in New York City, and my handsome son, Alex David, who is a talented writer and social media whiz for a movie and TV marketing company in L.A. You two mean the world to me and make me proud every minute of every day.

To my wife, Ann, with whom I wrote this book, thank you for taking this ride with me. More than anyone, you know how much I hate rollercoasters, but with you by my side, I know it's going to be okay. I love you, Annie. You are the best part of my life, my one and only.

Finally, I want to thank you, yes, YOU…the person who actually read this book. I hope somewhere along the way, on a page

or two, you picked up a little inspiration, a little encouragement, and a little trust in yourself to go after your dreams and to dream big. Then go out there and make it happen.

To all of you, I wish you 90% luck plus another 10% a lotta luck.

Joe Cipriano

Cast members of Primetime Voices For Children, the 31 voice actors I assembled to record our album of children's stories with all proceeds going to Mattel Children's Hospital UCLA.

Joan Baker	Anthony Mendez
Kay Bess	Paul Pape
Bob Bergen	Jim Pratt
Corey Burton	Bill Ratner
Joe Cipriano	Rino Romano
Howard Cogan	Scott Rummell
Townsend Coleman	Ashton Smith
Josh Daugherty	Jim Tasker
George DelHoyo	John Taylor
Kara Edwards	Randy Thomas
Dave Fennoy	Keri Tombazian
Pat Fraley	Sylvia Villagran
Stew Hererra	Rick Wasserman
Ben Patrick Johnson	Beau Weaver
Brian Lee	Zurek
Bill Lloyd	

We have a great group of people who were there from the beginning for the Don LaFontaine Voice-Over Lab at the Screen Actors Guild Foundation. Our advisory board members are:

Paul Pape, George Whittam and Joe Cipriano – co-founders

Advisory board: Townsend Coleman, Joshua Daugherty, George DelHoyo, Kevin Gershan, Vanessa Gilbert, Stew Herrera, Adam "Aejay'e" Jackson, Ben Patrick Johnson, Nita Whitaker LaFontaine, David Marc, Bill Ratner, Tony Rodgers, Rino Romano, Scott Rummell, Jim Tasker, Randy Thomas, Steve Tisherman, Sylvia Villagran, and Beau Weaver.

Other donors include: Brian Lee, Chris Corely and James Arnold Taylor, Chris Courrier at Sennheiser/Neumann Microphones, Tim Schweiger at Broadcast Supply Worldwide, MXL Microphones, IACF, DG Entertainment, Manley Laboratories, Shure Incorporated, and Auralex Acoustics.

The chairs and tables in the lab are sponsored as well.

Chairs: William Daniels, SBV Talent, Don Morrow, Dude Walker, Power & Twersky Business Management Group, Greg Chen, Lori Alan & Cedering Fox, Marla Boden, Janet M. Ault, John Osiecki (Bell Sound Studios), Adam & Linda Jackson, In memory of Danny Dark, Mary Grover, Zurek (Voice Over Universe), Ernie Anderson (SBV), Atlas Talent Agency, Steven Schwartz and Amy Gudelsky.

Tables: In memory of Phillip Patane, Sr., In memory of Cynthia Songe', TJ Jones in memory of Sue Thisdell Jones.

Our DLF lab administrator is Aric Shuford and our engineers are Mike Verela, Mickey Caputo and Rob Impala.

INDEX

About the Authors

Joe Cipriano is one of most successful voice-over artists in the country. He has worked for all of the major television networks and he has been the live announcer for such shows as The Primetime Emmy Awards, The Grammy Awards, plus many more live worldwide broadcasts. His list of credits include Food Network, Deal or No Deal, Hollywood Game Night, and America's Got Talent. Cipriano has contributed to several books about voice-over including "Secrets of Voice-Over Success" and "Voice for Hire." He is regarded as an expert in broadcasting and is featured in voice-over seminars from coast to coast. Cipriano received the Don LaFontaine Legacy Award for his charitable endeavors, professionalism, and longevity in the voice-over community. He lives in Los Angeles with his wife and co-author, Ann.

Ann Cipriano is an Emmy award winning television news writer and producer who worked at ABC News and NBC News. She was a producer on "The Tom Snyder Show" at KABC-TV in Los Angeles and also worked as a director for the syndicated show "Lifestyles of the Rich and Famous."